1998 P●RTLAND MUSEUM ●F ART BIENNIAL

Published in conjunction with the 1998

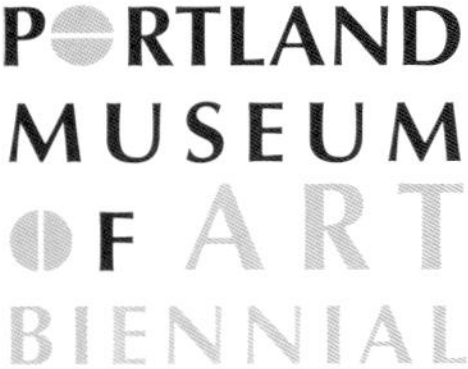

P●RTLAND MUSEUM ●F ART BIENNIAL

at the Portland Museum of Art, Maine,
November 5, 1998-January 3, 1999.

The *1998 Portland Museum of Art Biennial*
is made possible through the generous support
of anonymous donors. This exhibition catalogue
and the Jurors Prize are funded through a major
grant from the Wyeth Endowment for American Art.
Organization of the exhibition was supported
by the Maine Community Foundation.

The exhibition is sponsored by WGME 13.

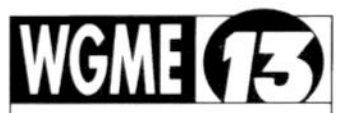

Cover images (top to bottom, left to right):
Michael Shaughnessy, *Pomoni's Loop and Fall, Second Variation*
(detail); Liv Kristen Robinson, *Belfast Waterfront (#5)* (detail);
Gail Spaien, *The Struggle Between the Intellect and the Spirit:
Just Before Deciding* (detail); Alan Bray, *Vernal Pond* (detail).

Reproduction photography by:
David Caras (Brackett, p. 12)
Benjamin Magro (Moore, p. 41)
Greg Morley (Zopp, p. 60)
Newbold Noyes III (Cashin McMillen, p. 17)
Robert Oliveira (Hunnibell, p. 34)
Adam Reich (Cady, p. 14)
Jay York (Campbell, p. 15, Gorvett, p. 25, Spaien, p. 51, Spencer, p. 52)
All other photographs are courtesy of the artist.

Designed by Karin Lundgren

Printed by Penmor Lithographers, Lewiston, Maine

Published by the Portland Museum of Art
Seven Congress Square, Portland, Maine 04101

Library of Congress Catalog Card Number: 98-67548

ISBN: 0-916857-16-6

MAINE IS THE LOCUS OF AN EXTRAORDINARY TRADITION OF CREATIVE ACHIEVEMENT IN THE VISUAL ARTS. For nearly two centuries, artists both native and "from away" have been inspired by the majesty of its landscape, the clarity of its northern light, and the opportunity its rural retreats afford to work free from distraction. It has nurtured the establishment of distinct art colonies and schools, which have, in turn, promoted a strong sense of community and the open exchange of ideas among artists. Maine and its artists can claim a vital role in the evolution of American art, from the origination of a national tradition of landscape painting to the rise of modernism, from the development of Abstract Expressionism to the revitalization of realist painting.

This is not a dormant tradition. The continuing vitality of Maine's creative communities is the impetus behind the *1998 Portland Museum of Art Biennial*, the first in what will become a tradition of stimulating exhibitions of contemporary art. The goal of the *Biennial* is to present an enlightening cross-section of the best work produced during the past two years by artists who have spent all or part of their time in Maine. Our call for entries was met with submissions from 914 artists. This gratifying response confirmed the need for a Maine showcase for the work of the painters, sculptors, photographers, printmakers, and others who contribute to the state's artistic vitality. We hope that our efforts to provide such a forum will be met as enthusiastically by artists in future years.

Our panel of jurors ably rose to the challenge of selecting the 88 works by 56 artists included here. Renowned artist Will Barnet; Rachel Rosenfield Lafo, senior curator at the DeCordova Museum and Sculpture Park in Lincoln, Massachusetts; and Bridget Moore of the DC Moore Gallery in New York City brought their trained eyes, extensive knowledge of contemporary art, and inexhaustible patience to the blind jurying process. The result is a strong selection of recent work that confirms Maine's sustained and sustaining place in American art. The *1998 Portland Museum of Art Biennial* offers a glimpse into the great diversity of the artists who are drawn to Maine. Works by artists who have spent their lives and careers in Maine are exhibited beside pieces created during or as a result of seasonal visits to the state. The enriching role of Maine's art schools is represented by the accomplished work of faculty members at the University of Maine, the Maine College of Art, and the Skowhegan School of Painting and Sculpture, as well as by students of those institutions. What emerges is a view of Maine as a creative touchstone for a local, regional, and national community of artists.

Similarly, this exhibition reflects the efforts of the dedicated community of people that create and sustain the Portland Museum of Art's programs. As with all of this Museum's exhibitions, the *1998 Biennial* is the result of the hard work of our full staff. Jessica Nicoll, chief curator; Aprile Gallant, curator of prints, drawings, and photographs; and Jessica Skwire, curatorial assistant, led the process of making our vision of this exhibition a reality. The crucial work of coordinating all communications with, and materials submitted by, artists was handled with grace, professionalism, and good humor by our Biennial Intern, Julia Kirby. Our Registrar, Beverly Parsons, effortlessly facilitated the receipt of artwork, and our preparators, Stuart Hunter and Gregory Welch, installed it with equal elegance and ease. This catalogue is the product of the creative skills of our graphic designer, Karin Lundgren, and her assistant, Teresa Lagrange.

None of this work would have been possible without the leadership of several crucial supporters. We are enormously grateful for the generosity of the anonymous donors who share our vision of the Portland Museum of Art as a gathering place and resource for Maine's artists. The Maine Community Foundation underwrote the Biennial Internship, providing the *1998 Biennial* with a dedicated staff member who has had an invaluable learning experience. Thanks are also due to the Wyeth family and the other Trustees of the Wyeth Endowment for American Art for underscoring their commitment to contemporary art by funding this catalogue and the Jurors Prize. Finally, our appreciation also goes to WGME 13 whose sponsorship of the exhibition materially supports the arts in our community.

DANIEL E. O'LEARY, DIRECTOR

JURORS STATEMENTS

WILL BARNET
ARTIST

I found it a pleasure to be able to judge the wide array of talent that those associated with Maine had to offer. It was interesting to see the proliferation of styles and various mediums of expression, for the most part reflecting a lively awareness of the contemporary world of art. I was somewhat surprised that many of the works were not reflective of Maine landscapes, possibly due to contemporary trends, in addition to a pervasive lack of structure and imagery that relied too heavily on the subjective. In my own personal judgement, I looked for a certain formal order regardless of style and often found concurrence with my fellow jurors. I am grateful for the wide range of assistance that was offered by the Museum's staff, whose efforts eased our labor.

RACHEL ROSENFIELD LAFO
SENIOR CURATOR, DeCORDOVA MUSEUM AND SCULPTURE PARK, LINCOLN, MA

It was a great honor to be asked to be a juror for the *1998 Portland Museum of Art Biennial* exhibition. I was already familiar with the work of many artists working in Maine, but I was curious to see who would submit and whether there would be a large contingent of what some consider to be the prototypical Maine image—a clearly delineated landscape with a house overlooking meadow or water. Indeed, there were quite a few realist landscapes to choose from, but also submitted were landscapes of a more spiritual or metaphorical turn, abstractions both geometric and gestural, and an interesting selection of sculpture made out of materials as diverse as nails, reeds, cypress, slate, and paper.

The range of work submitted indicates that Maine's vital art community draws upon many sources—from those who live and work there on a full-time basis to those who visit Maine for shorter periods of time. The artists' interest in the observed environment, formal issues, art historical references, and conceptual conceits reflect concerns in contemporary art.

BRIDGET MOORE
DC MOORE GALLERY, NEW YORK

As a native of Maine, I was pleased to return and join Rachel Lafo and Will Barnet to view more than 7,000 slides submitted for this first *Portland Museum of Art Biennial* exhibition. I have always retained roots here but after nearly two decades immersed in the New York art world, I was proud to see such strong and diverse work being produced in Maine.

It was our intention to select what we felt were the strongest works submitted in all media, given the natural limitations of jurying through slides. Just as all good art conveys multiple meanings, so does art evolve from multiple methods. We were pleased to see such a flowering of varied expressions.

While the choices were difficult, we hope this exhibition is part of the ongoing exploration and celebration of contemporary art in Maine.

BORN: 1948, Torrington, CT   RESIDENCE: Newton, MA (Summer Residence: Georgetown, ME)

DANTE'S WOODS #2
1995-97
oil on panel
60 x 48 inches

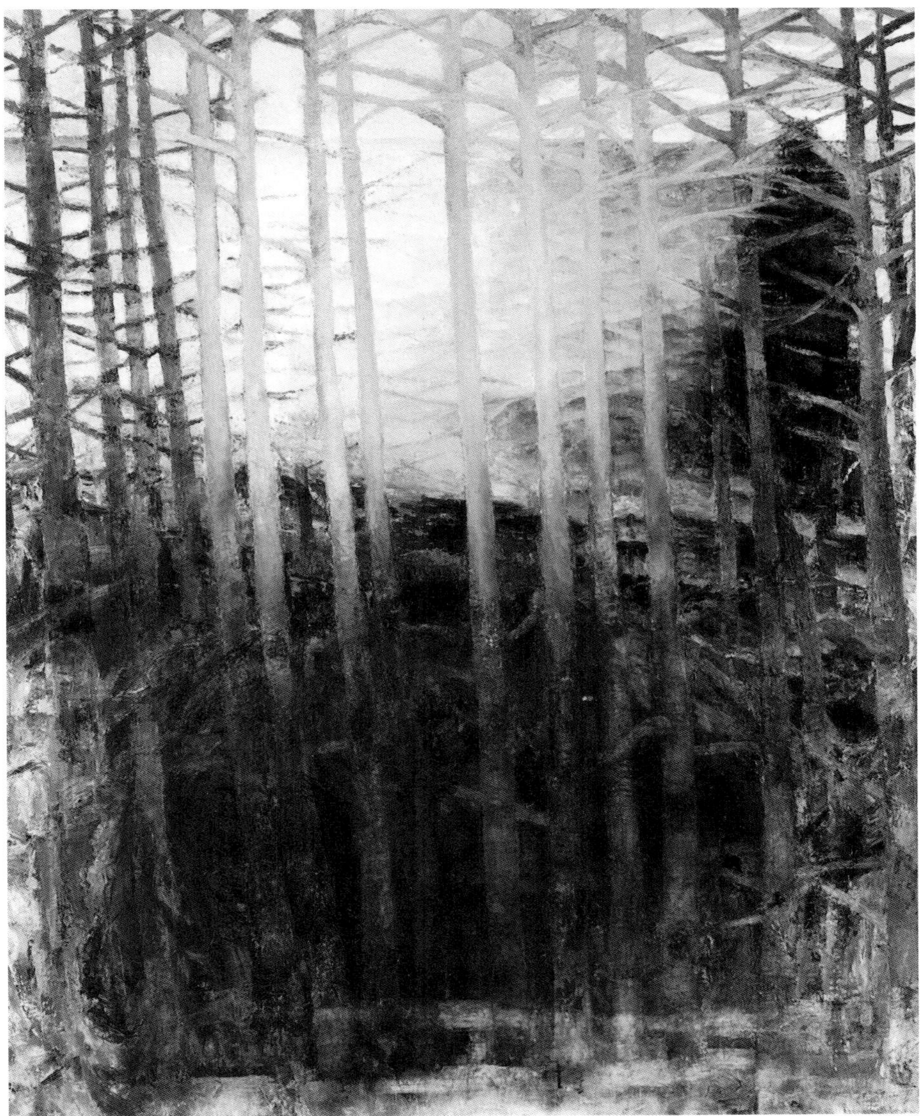

EDUCATION

1977   Skowhegan School of Painting and
        Sculpture, Maine
1976   Masters of Education, Lesley College,
        Cambridge, Massachusetts
1972   B.F.A., Boston University, School of
        Visual Arts

HONORS AND AWARDS

1995   Fellowship, Balinglen Arts Foundation,
        Ballycastle, County Mayo, Ireland
1995   Individual Grant for Works on Paper,
        New England Foundation for the Arts

SELECTED SOLO EXHIBITIONS

1993   Victoria Munroe Gallery, New York
1991-92 Felicita Foundation, Escondido, California

SELECTED GROUP EXHIBITIONS

1997   *Land and Body*, University of Florida Art
        Gallery, Gainesville
1996   *Skowhegan at 50: The Maine Legacy*, Maine
        Coast Artists, Rockport, and Baxter Gallery,
        Maine College of Art, Portland
1995   *Inspired by Nature: A Contemporary View*,
        Boston College Museum of Art, Chestnut
        Hill, Massachusetts
1995,   *The Armstrongs: Three Generations*, The
        Rose Gallery, Kent, Connecticut (also 1994
        and 1993)
1994   *A Gallery Retrospective*, California Center
        for the Arts, Escondido

SELECTED COLLECTIONS

- Federal Reserve Bank, Massachusetts
- Fidelity Investments, Massachusetts
- DeCordova Museum and Sculpture Park,
  Lincoln, Massachusetts

I grew up on an inland farm. My mother died suddenly when I was five. After that I spent most of my free time outside, playing in the fields and woods and down by the river. I was a solitary child, living far from town and society. I learned to fill my time with nature. I sought both solace and adventure from her, and eventually passion and revelation.

I learned to be alone and to experience landscape as a visionary world. When it came time to choose an occupation, painting chose me I think because it was such a natural way to manifest that rapture. Now I live near Boston in the winter and on the coast of Maine in the summer. I have been on the Fine Arts faculty at Boston College since 1989. I have stayed with painting all these years because it's the best way for me to express the ecstasy I experience when I am alone with nature. Contradictions abound, blasting me into the metaphysical; rocks are alive, light has weight, and thought becomes matter. The coast of Maine is an ecstatic place, full of highly charged visual events. My painting, *Dante's Woods #2*, is inspired by Maine.

MARY ARO

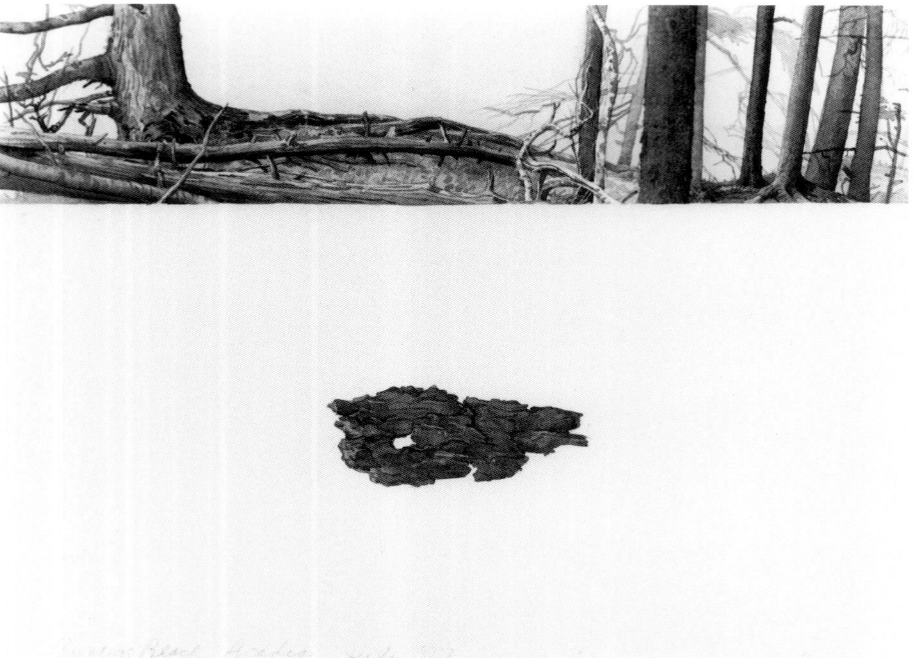

HUNTERS BEACH, ACADIA
1997
watercolor on paper
12 x 16 inches

EDUCATION

1982   M.F.A., Wayne State University, Detroit, Michigan
1980   B.F.A., Wayne State University

SELECTED GROUP EXHIBITIONS

1996   *Annual Juried Exhibition*, Maine Coast Artists, Rockport
1996   *Michigan Fine Arts Competition*, Birmingham Bloomfield Art Association
1996   *Patrimonio*, Wayne State University
1995   *Aspects of Realism*, Traveling Exhibition, Hillsdale College, Michigan
1995   *49th Annual Michigan Watercolor Exhibition*, Art Center of Battle Creek

SELECTED COLLECTIONS

- Springfield Art Museum, Missouri
- Ameritech, Detroit

When painting outdoors, sitting for hours in one location, I feel I become part of the landscape. Before me I see infinite shapes, forms, colors, and textures; transferring what I see to a flat piece of paper is totally absorbing. My interests in form and composition have led me to combine the realism of my landscapes and still lifes with abstraction. The white paper becomes a foil on which geometric shapes, such as a rectangle (often a landscape) and a trapezoid (often a table) are placed. The abstract shapes that the objects create and the white space of the paper are as important as the realistic objects themselves.

My interest is in the interplay of the abstract forms and the specific objects and places depicted within these forms. In creating these compositions I allow content and meaning to evolve intuitively. Smaller paintings sometimes have an object from the ground around the painting site added to the lower portion of the painting. At other times the lower section is left empty, emphasizing the rectangular landscape above—a simple horizontal shape—a line of peace and harmony.

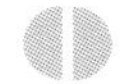

TARGET III
1996
monotype
180 x 144 inches

EDUCATION

1996   M.F.A., School of the Museum of Fine Arts, Boston, and Tufts University, Medford, Massachusetts

1979   B.F.A., Design, Syracuse University, New York

HONORS AND AWARDS

1997-98 Residency, Frans Masereel, Flemish Ministry of Culture, Kasterlee, Belgium

1997   Fulbright Memorial Fund, Teacher Alternate to Japan

1996-97 Residency, Cité Internationale des Arts, Paris

1996   *Bridge Opera IV*, Award and honorarium, C.A.G.E., Cincinnati, Ohio

1995   Residency and exhibition, Ulappa 95, International Art Symposium, Turku, Finland

SELECTED SOLO EXHIBITIONS

1998   *Arrow Opera*, print installation with sound art, Gallery 68 ELF, Cologne, Germany

1998   *You Haven't Words*, Frans Masereel, Flemish Ministry of Culture, Kasterlee

1997   *Desire*, Cité Internationale des Arts

1996   *Bridge Opera IV*, Installation with performance, C.A.G.E.

1996   *100 Bridges Opera III*, Installation with shortwave radio broadcast from Croatia, Tisch Gallery, Tufts University

SELECTED GROUP EXHIBITIONS

1997   *Twenty-fifth Anniversary Exhibition*, Flemish Ministry of Culture, Antwerp

1996   *Annual Print Exhibition* (one of ten international artists chosen for catalogue), Flemish Ministry of Culture, Kasterlee

1995   *Twelve Invited International Artists*, Galleria Just, Turku

1995   *Nuremburg 95*, Tour of part of Cracow International Print Triennial, Nuremburg, Germany

1994   *Degrees of Assimilation: Art from Diverse Cultures*, Rhode Island College, Providence

SELECTED COLLECTIONS

- Royal Museum of the Fine Arts, Antwerp
- Thorn Industries, Boston and London

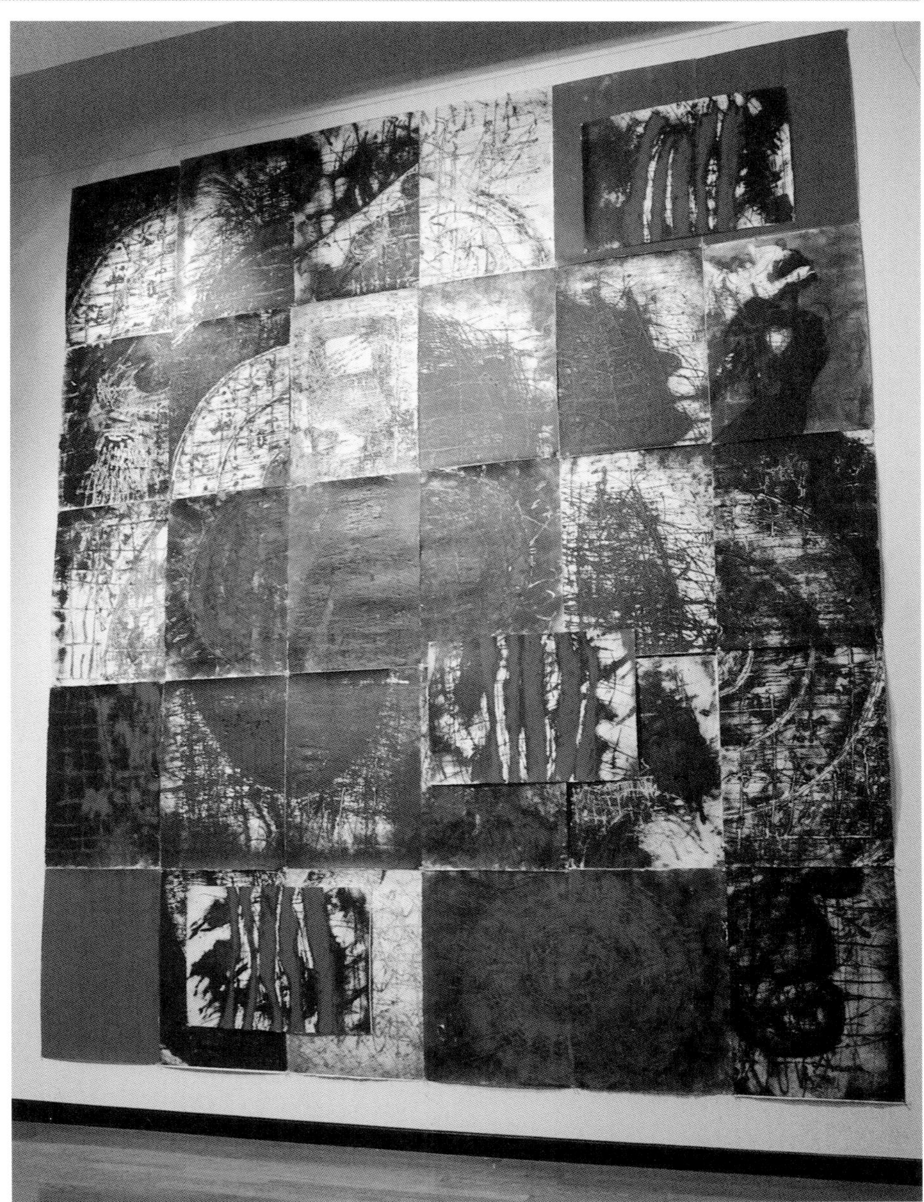

My work is about conflict. I am thinking of the forces or needs that will make one side interact or even fight another. There is sound and music and architecture. On many levels my work has been about war. My only power to deal with it has been through art.

JEFFERY BECTON

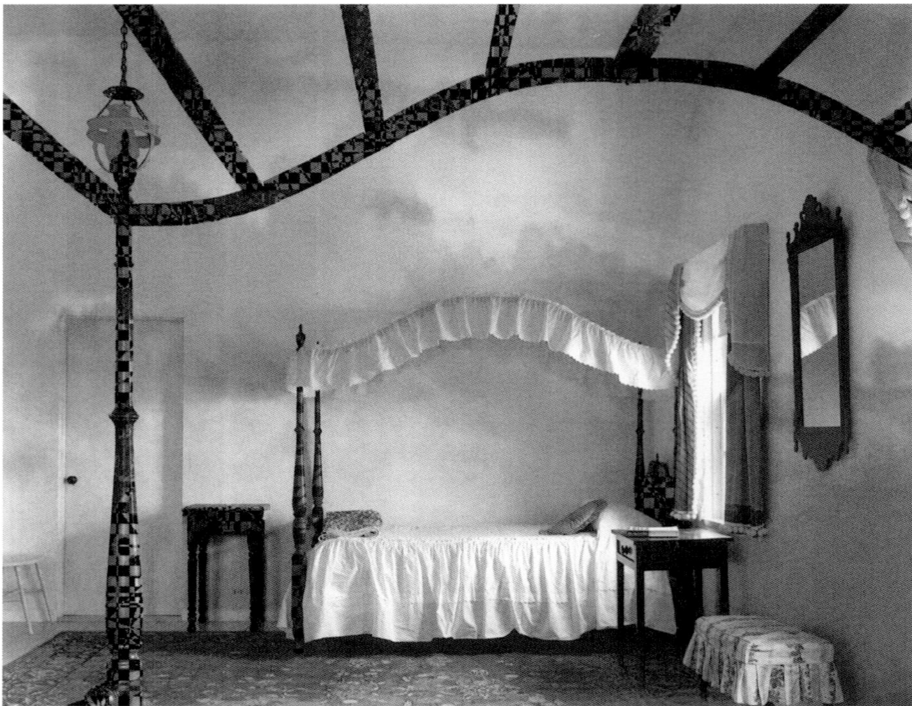

ANTICIPATING ASCENSION
1997
Iris print
16 x 23 inches

Although I have been working in design, black-and-white photography, and using computers since 1984, it was not until 1992 that improvements in technology enabled me to explore and find expression in a rich new vocabulary. The advent of high resolution, continuous tone, digital color technology has enabled me to create images of remarkable precision, facilitating the juxtaposition of loose, free, painterly elements with tight, hard-edged, photographic realism. The computer technology I employ both fosters and gives form to visual ambiguities. Within this new medium, the ability to blur the boundaries of mixed media has permitted me to reinvestigate that realm in which places serve as metaphors for states of being.

EDUCATION
1976   M.F.A., Graphic Design, Yale University School of Art, New Haven, Connecticut
1973-74 Special Student, Yale University School of Art
1970   B.A., History, Yale University

HONORS AND AWARDS
1976   Alice G. K. Garland Prize for excellence in the second year, Yale University School of Art

SELECTED SOLO EXHIBITIONS
1997   Turtle Gallery, Deer Isle, Maine
1995   DIAA Gallery, Deer Isle

SELECTED GROUP EXHIBITIONS
1998   *20th Annual Juried Show*, Maine Coast Artists, Rockport
1998   *Landscapes*, Digital Photography 98, juried, Bradley University, Peoria, Illinois
1996   *Nash's Greatest Hits*, The Photographers Gallery, London
1996   *Celebrating the New Space*, Turtle Gallery
1995   *Annual Juried Show*, Maine Coast Artists

SELECTED COLLECTIONS
- New Orleans Museum of Art, Louisiana
- United Technologies Inc., Hartford
- Becton-Dickinson Inc., Franklin Lakes, New Jersey

BORN: 1974, Lewiston, ME   **RESIDENCE:** Brunswick, ME

DICHOTOMY
1998
marker on wood

EDUCATION

1997-98 McGill University, Montréal, Canada
1994-96 University of Southern Maine, Gorham
1993-94 Rochester Institute of Technology, New York

This piece is constructed from the materials that I collect on the streets of Portland: trash items, unwanted items, abstract signs, and clear but invisible messages that surround what I believe myself and others of today are a part of. They are simple and accessible for the viewer and offer a symbol for anyone who looks within. The constant motion of the signs and symbols allows few to leave without a reflection or thought which depicts the external or internal world that they live in. This piece represents the idea that all items in our world, over time, participate in entropy. So touch, add, subtract, or misuse this construction, because if it is destroyed I will gladly pick up the pieces and construct something that contains more.

BRETT BIGBEE

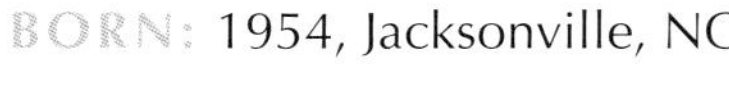

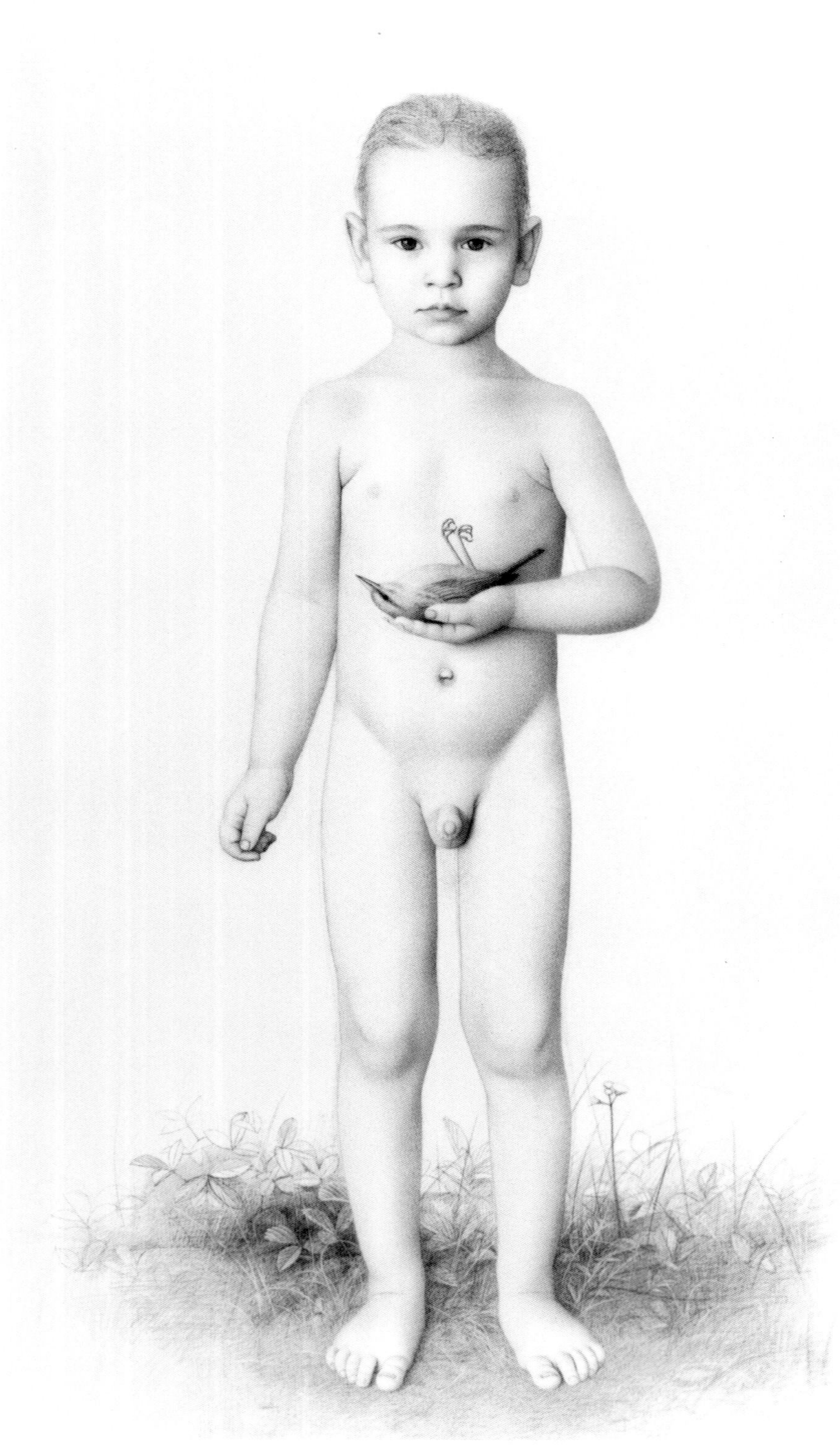

BIRD I
1998
graphite on paper
48¼ x 28¼ inches

EDUCATION
1985　Pennsylvania Academy of the Fine
　　　Arts, Philadelphia

HONORS AND AWARDS
1997　Catherine Gibbons Granger Award in Painting,
　　　Pennsylvania Academy of the Fine Arts
1994　Richard and Hinda Rosenthal Foundation
　　　Award, American Academy of Arts and
　　　Letters, New York

SELECTED SOLO EXHIBITIONS
1999　New Britain Museum of American Art,
　　　Connecticut
1999　Tibor de Nagy Gallery, New York
　　　(tentatively scheduled to travel to The Butler
　　　Institute of American Art, Youngstown, Ohio)
1996　Terry Dintenfass in association
　　　with Salander-O'Reilly Galleries,
　　　New York
1994　*PERSPECTIVES: Brett Bigbee Paintings and
　　　Drawings, 1989-1993*, Portland Museum of
　　　Art, Maine
1993　Fischbach Gallery, New York

SELECTED GROUP EXHIBITIONS
1998　*Invitational Drawing Exhibition*, Arkansas
　　　Arts Center, Little Rock
1997　*The Figure*, Tibor de Nagy Gallery
1997　*Unbroken Line*, Centennial Exhibition of the
　　　Fellowship of the Pennsylvania Academy of
　　　the Fine Arts
1997　*Realism in 20th Century American Painting*,
　　　Ogunquit Museum of American Art, Maine
1996　*Self-Portraits*, Edith Caldwell Gallery,
　　　San Francisco

SELECTED COLLECTIONS
- Arnot Art Museum, Elmira, New York
- Bowdoin College Museum of Art,
  Brunswick, Maine
- Farnsworth Art Museum, Rockland, Maine
- Ogunquit Museum of American Art
- Portland Museum of Art

HUSK
1997
welded nails
22 x 48 x 42 inches

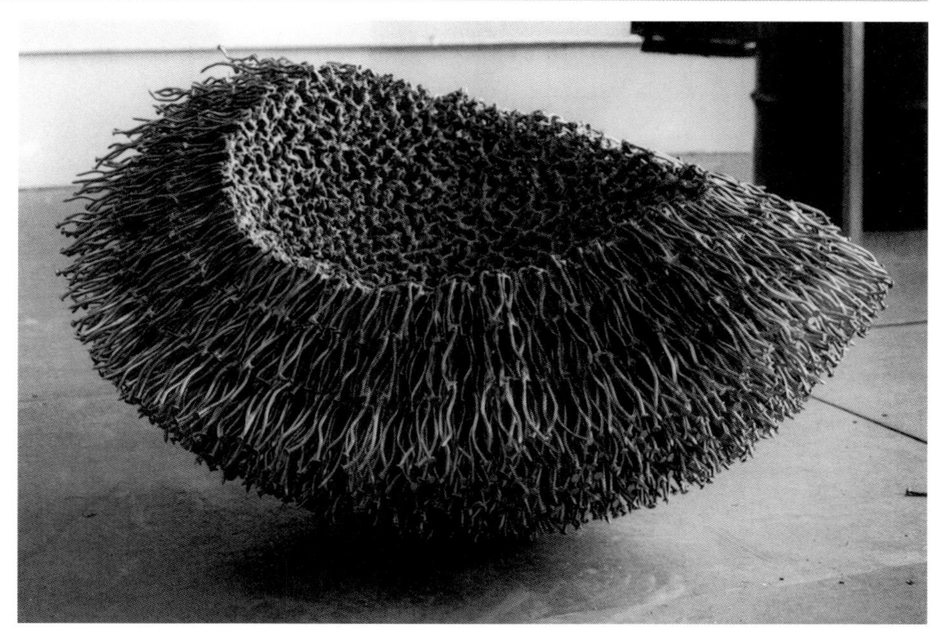

The rhythm of making is my physical mantra.

EDUCATION

1992 Skowhegan School of Painting and
Sculpture, Maine
1990 B.F.A., Alfred University, New York

HONORS AND AWARDS

1995-96 Artists Residency, The MacDowell Colony
for the Arts, Peterborough, New Hampshire
1994 Artists Residency, Yaddo, Saratoga Springs,
New York

SELECTED SOLO EXHIBITIONS

1998 *Winter Works*, Maine Coast Artists, Rockport
1997 *Frozen By Fire*, Bowdoin College Museum of
Art, Brunswick, Maine
1996 *Recent Gatherings*, Pulliam-Deffenbaugh
Gallery, Portland, Oregon
1995 *Five Years*, Chase Gallery, Spokane,
Washington
1993 *Evidence in Sculpture*, Wichita Center for
the Arts, Kansas

SELECTED GROUP EXHIBITIONS

1997 *Four on the Floor*, Icon Contemporary Art,
Brunswick, Maine
1997 *The Maine Coast Artists Invitational*
1996 *Pure Form*, Portland Institute for
Contemporary Art, Oregon
1995 *Interior Idioms*, Seafirst Gallery, Seattle,
Washington
1994 *Gallery Artists*, Pulliam-Deffenbaugh
Gallery

SELECTED COLLECTIONS

- Microsoft Corporations, Redmond,
Washington
- Hugo Neu Corporations, New York

PRILLA SMITH BRACKETT

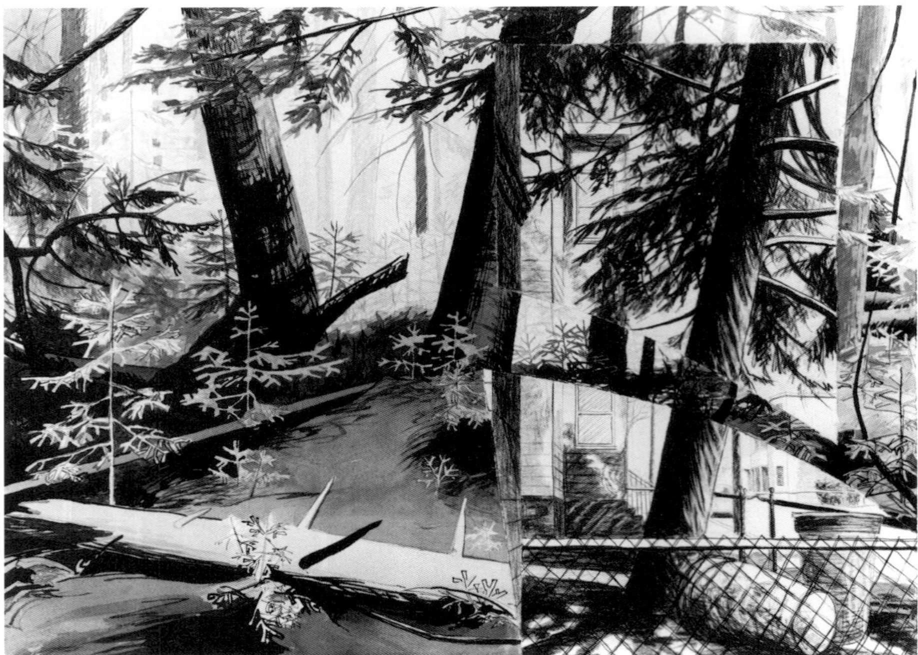

REMNANTS: COMMUNION #8
1998
acrylic wash, graphite, conté, charcoal, pastel,
and collage on paper
26¼ x 34⅛ inches

Our view of wilderness is rooted in our 20th-century consciousness. We see resource, recreation, and opportunity where once we saw beauty. My work explores this view, depicting the precarious existence of northern New England old-growth forests. I present barriers and fractured images as metaphors for our abuse of the environment and for our lives so removed from the natural world. At the same time, it is important to express the mystery and feeling which initially inspired me. In other pieces, I explore the parallels and contrasts between northern old-growth forests and urban trees, suggesting the struggle between freedom and constraint. Throughout, I try to express the spiritual energy and sensual power of trees.

I have been working on this project for over two years, using photos taken while hiking and camping in pockets of old-growth forests in northern Maine. In the work from this time span I've experimented variously with different ways of creating a subtle sense of disjuncture or disequilibrium. Some strategies include: juxtaposing two sets of images; collaging paper or canvas panels onto the canvas to create a physical difference, treating the fragmented panels differently from the rest of the image; and using unstable panels which have been torn to represent a fragmented image. However, if the viewer senses disjuncture or disequilibrium but has an interpretation other than an environmental one, I am happy for the multiple possibilities.

Another way I've worked with landscape images is represented in this body of work: combining many small pieces to make a larger whole. In the studio, with close-up images from both the old-growth forest and the urban setting, I work with spatial and temporal multiplicity, within an overarching unity, so that the relationships between the canvases are as important as the images alone.

EDUCATION

1981 M.F.A., Drawing and Painting, University of Nebraska, Lincoln

1967 M.A., Sociology, University of California, Berkeley

1964 B.A., Sociology/Psychology, Sarah Lawrence College, Bronxville, New York

HONORS AND AWARDS

1998 Lois Neelie Gill Award and Residency, Ucross Foundation, Clearmont, Wyoming

1998-97 Residency, Ragdale Foundation, Lake Forest, Illinois

1997 Second Place, Cash Award, *National Juried Exhibition*, Lancaster Museum of Art, Pennsylvania

1994 Residency, The Francine Frank Fellow, The Millay Colony of The Arts, Austerlitz, New York

1991-92 Earthwatch Artist Award, Earthwatch, Watertown, Massachusetts

SELECTED SOLO EXHIBITIONS

1994 *Two Hemispheres: Drawing & Paintings*, Gallery 57, Cambridge, Massachusetts

1993 *Marking a Year*, DeCordova Museum and Sculpture Park, Lincoln, Massachusetts

SELECTED GROUP EXHIBITIONS

1998 *Here There & Everywhere: Group Landscape Show*, Creiger-Dane Gallery, Boston

1998 *New England/New Talent*, Fitchburg Art Museum, Massachusetts

1998 *Creative Responses to Global Warnings*, Richard F. Brush Art Gallery, St. Lawrence University, Canton, New York

1997 *The Drawing Show*, Boston Center for the Arts, Mills Gallery

SELECTED COLLECTIONS:

- Fogg Art Museum, Harvard University Art Museums, Cambridge, Massachusetts
- DeCordova Museum and Sculpture Park
- Art in U.S. Embassies Program, Washington, DC
- National Museum of Women in the Arts, Washington, DC
- Boston Public Library

VERNAL POND
1997
casein on panel
26 x 34 inches

EDUCATION

1973   M.F.A., Painting, Villa Schifanoia,
Florence, Italy

1971   University of Southern Maine, Gorham

1968   Art Institute of Boston, Massachusetts

SELECTED SOLO EXHIBITIONS

1996   Schmidt Bingham Gallery, New York

1994   Maine Coast Artists, Rockport

1993   *PERSPECTIVES: Alan Bray: Redefining
Landscape*, Portland Museum of Art, Maine

1992   *Painted Places: Graphic Images*, Gleason
Fine Arts, Portland, Maine

SELECTED GROUP EXHIBITIONS

1996   *Destiny Manifest: American Landscape
Painting in the Nineties*, Samuel P. Harn
Museum of Art, University of Florida,
Gainesville

1996   *Are You Blue?*, Schmidt Bingham Gallery

1993   *Night Light*, Barn Gallery, Ogunquit, Maine

1993   *40th Anniversary Exhibition*, Ogunquit
Museum of American Art, Maine

1992-93 *On the Edge: Forty Years of Maine Painting*,
Maine Coast Artists

1992   *Art of Maine: A Bounty of Woods and Water*,
Monmouth Museum, Lincroft, New Jersey

SELECTED COLLECTIONS

- Farnsworth Art Museum, Rockland, Maine
- Fruit of the Loom/Farley Inc., Chicago
- Portland Museum of Art
- Maine Savings Bank Collection (now
Citibank), Portland
- Memphis Cancer Center, Tennessee

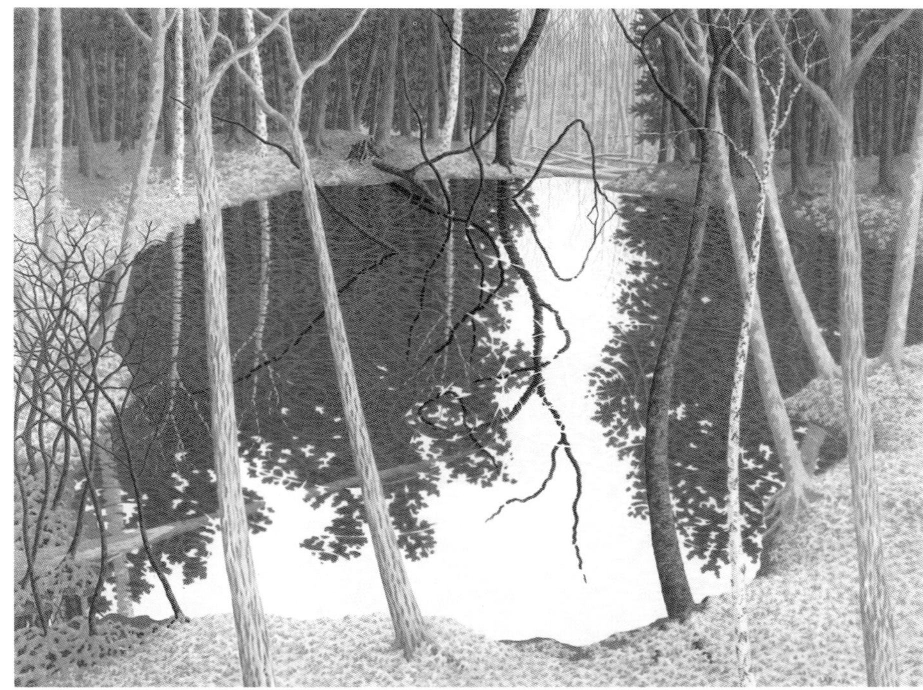

I become interested in a place or a phenomenon through familiarity. The
experience of being in nature is a complex relationship. The scene is only
one aspect; our sense of being a part of what we are experiencing is the more
compelling aspect, and this lies in the fabric of remembrance, dream, and
affection. It is through an accretion of these values and the particulars of
place that I find an image.

SAM CADY

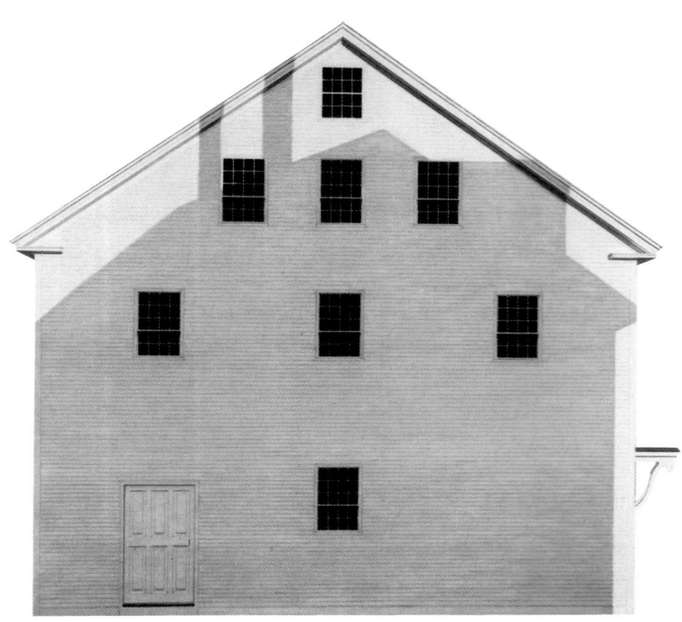

TWO SHAKER BUILDINGS, EARLY EVENING
1998
oil on shaped canvas
62 x 67 x 1½ inches

Two Shaker Buildings, Early Evening is part of a recent group of paintings depicting different faces of architecture, from massive, opaque office towers to slapped-together ice fishing shanties. With the aim of purveying different spirits or psychologies of architecture, the work reflects various aspects of life from occupational to domestic, recreational to spiritual, past to future, and different moods, from humorous to severe to meditative. For me the Shaker buildings were quiet and soothing.

EDUCATION

1967　M.F.A., Indiana University, Bloomington
1965　B.A., University of New Hampshire, Durham

SELECTED SOLO EXHIBITIONS

1998　*Architecture, Recent Paintings by Sam Cady*, Mary Ryan Gallery, New York
1997　Caldbeck Gallery, Rockland, Maine
1996　Howard Yezerski Gallery, Boston
1995　Barbara Gillman Gallery, Miami Beach, Florida
1994　Mary Ryan Gallery

SELECTED GROUP EXHIBITIONS

1998　*Masters of the Masters: Faculty of the Master of Fine Arts Program*, School of Visual Arts, The Butler Institute of American Art, Youngstown, Ohio
1997　*Prize Goods: Art and Artifacts Captured for the Collections*, Peabody-Essex Museum, Salem, Massachusetts
1995　*Structures*, Mary Ryan Gallery
1995　*On the Waterfront*, Maine Coast Artists, Rockport
1995　*DeCordova Collects*, DeCordova Museum and Sculpture Park, Lincoln, Massachusetts

SELECTED COLLECTIONS

- Addison Gallery of American Art, Andover, Massachusetts
- DeCordova Museum and Sculpture Park
- Pacific Securities International, Los Angeles
- The Peabody-Essex Museum
- United Central Bank of Denver, Colorado

THE FAMILY
1996-98
charcoal, conté, and graphite on paper
33 x 40 inches

EDUCATION

1961 — Art Students League, New York

SELECTED SOLO EXHIBITIONS

1995 — The Bergen Museum of Art and Science, Paramus, New Jersey

SELECTED GROUP EXHIBITIONS

1996 — Two Person Drawing Show with Lloyd Goldsmith, Gerold Wunderlich Gallery, New York

1996 — *2nd Annual Lana International Art Competition*, Kismet Gallery, San Jose, California

1996 — *171st Annual Exhibition*, National Academy of Design, New York

1996 — *Rediscovering the Landscape of the Americas*, Gerald Peters Gallery, Santa Fe, New Mexico

1996 — *The Future of the Past: 15 Contemporary Realists Paint Boston*, Boston Athenaeum

SELECTED COLLECTIONS

- Museum of Fine Arts, Boston
- Metropolitan Museum of Art, New York
- Boston Public Library
- Chemical Bank, New York
- Eastern Gas, Boston

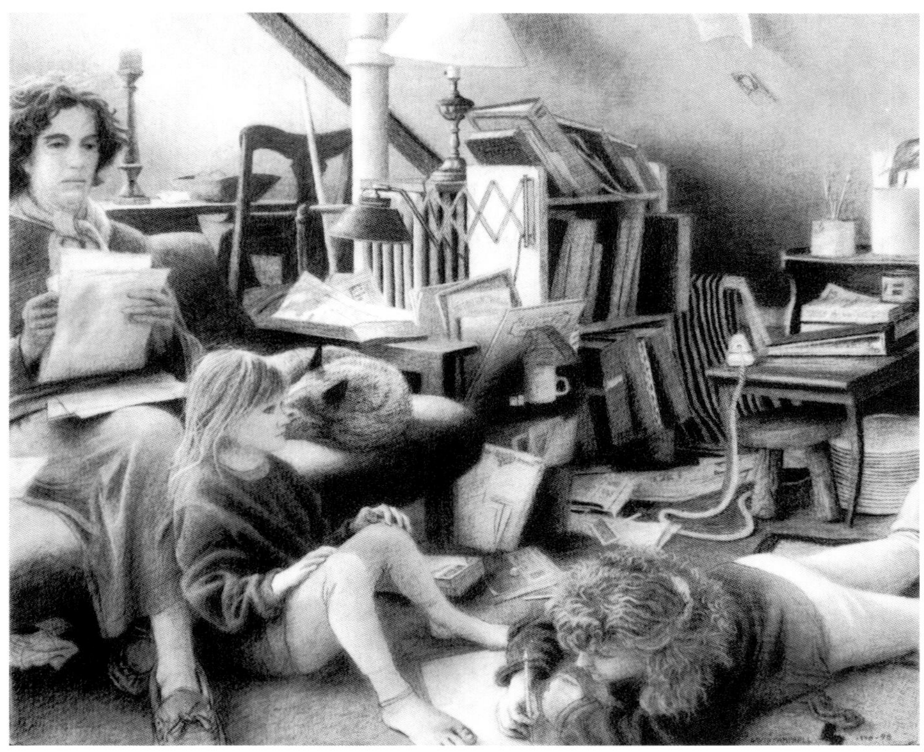

I paint and draw from life in my surroundings—landscapes and interiors.

◑ PATRICIA CAMPBELL

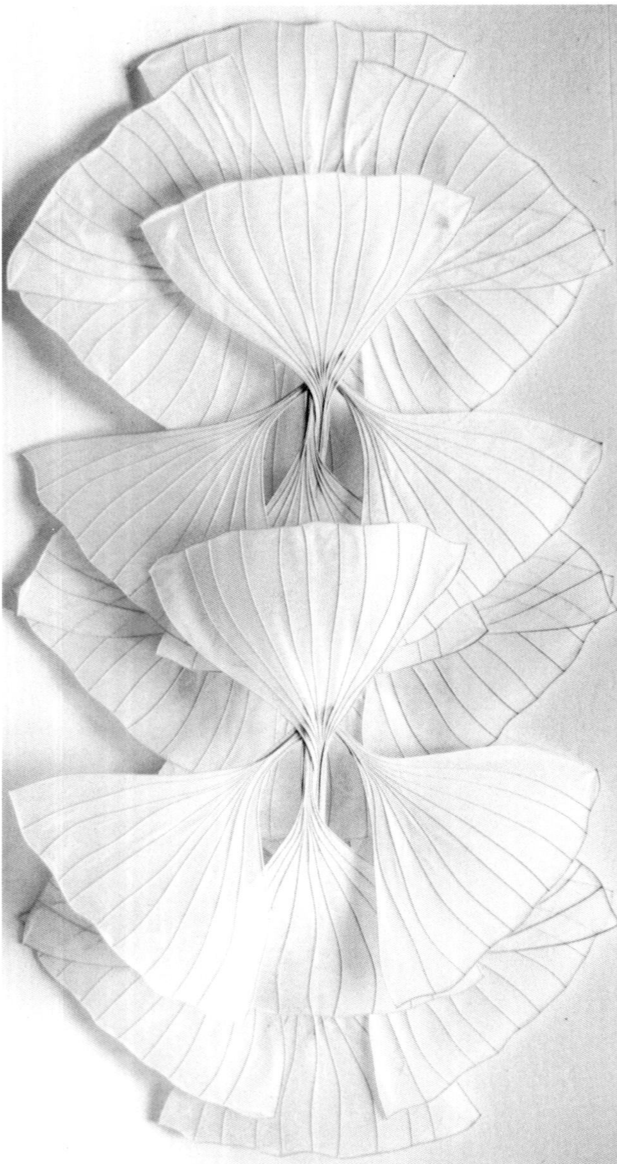

CONSTRUCTED FORM (LOTUS)
1998
rice paper and reed
62 x 34 x 4 inches

EDUCATION

1978   M.F.A., Fiber, Cranbrook Academy of Art, Bloomfield Hills, Michigan
1971   M.F.A., Textiles, University of Georgia, Athens
1965   B.A., Art History, Colby College, Waterville, Maine

SELECTED GROUP EXHIBITIONS

1997   *SOFA Chicago 1997*, Brown/Grotta Gallery, Wilton, Connecticut
1997   *The 10th Wave Part I: New Baskets and Freestanding Fiber Sculpture*, Brown/Grotta Gallery
1996   *Surface to Structure*, Greenville Museum of Art, North Carolina
1996   Artspace, Raleigh, North Carolina
1993   Long House Museum, East Hampton, New York

SELECTED COLLECTIONS

- York Elementary School, Maine
- Aetna Life Insurance Company, Hartford, Connecticut
- University of Southern Maine, Portland
- School of Law, University of Connecticut, Hartford
- Marina Square, Singapore

Process and image are closely associated and variations on a single theme. I became an artist initially because of being born into a family intensely concerned with the craft movement. I learned at an early age that I enjoyed the meditative process of making. I chose to study textiles because the process and the final image (the making of the warp and the structuring of the woven plane) are rhythmical. I no longer use a loom. The materials have changed. The structure is now, at times, made of steel. The working rhythmical repeat of form, however, remains constant.

The investigation and the image continue to evolve with variations. It is my belief that all of this is one single expression; that we, as artists, while working, reach for the universal image, as Jung has written. Through different interpretations of the image, we come to new understandings of ourselves and our relationship with the universe.

BORN: Chicago, IL

RESIDENCE: Marlboro, ME

UNTITLED NO. 20
1996
oil on canvas
92 x 72 inches

EDUCATION
1966   B.A., Art History/Sculpture, Bard College, Annandale, New York

SELECTED SOLO EXHIBITIONS
1997   *New Paintings*, Lakes Gallery and Sculpture Garden, South Casco, Maine
1995   *New Paintings*, Frick Gallery, Belfast, Maine
1994   Area Gallery, University of Southern Maine, Portland

SELECTED GROUP EXHIBITIONS
1996   *The Grid Revealed and Veiled*, Maine Coast Artists, Rockport
1995   *Three Abstract Artists: New Work*, Lakes Gallery and Sculpture Garden
1994   *Abstractions II*, Frick Gallery
1994   *Going for a Walk with a Line*, Union of Maine Visual Artists, Mount Desert
1994   *Annual Juried Exhibition*, Maine Coast Artists

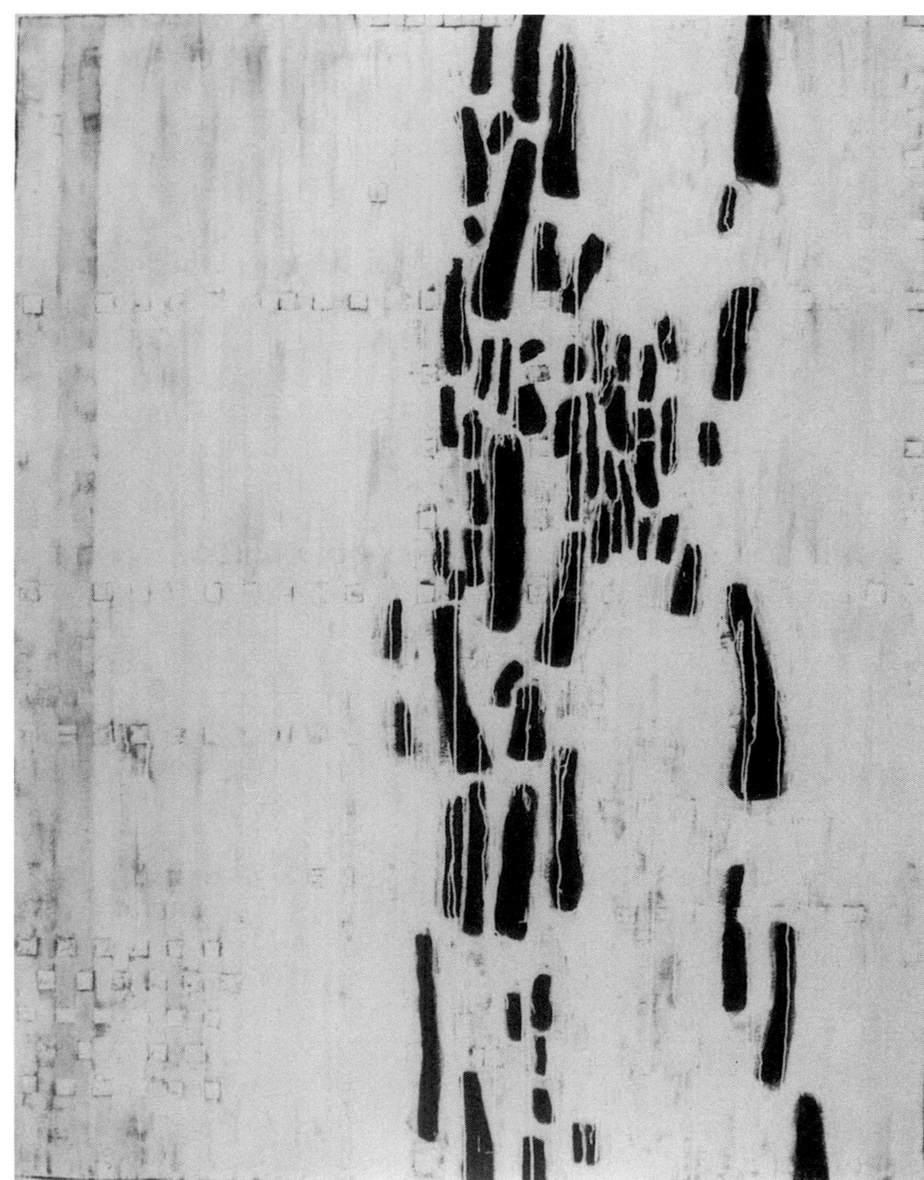

Making a painting is using order and paint to pass through the "eye of a needle." The method of getting through is a discourse in risk, an encounter of conflicts.

The rules are not explicit.

The losses are often painful.

Through the eye, the painting comes to a dialogue with the viewer.

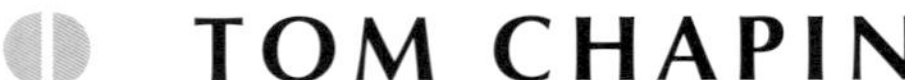

TOM CHAPIN

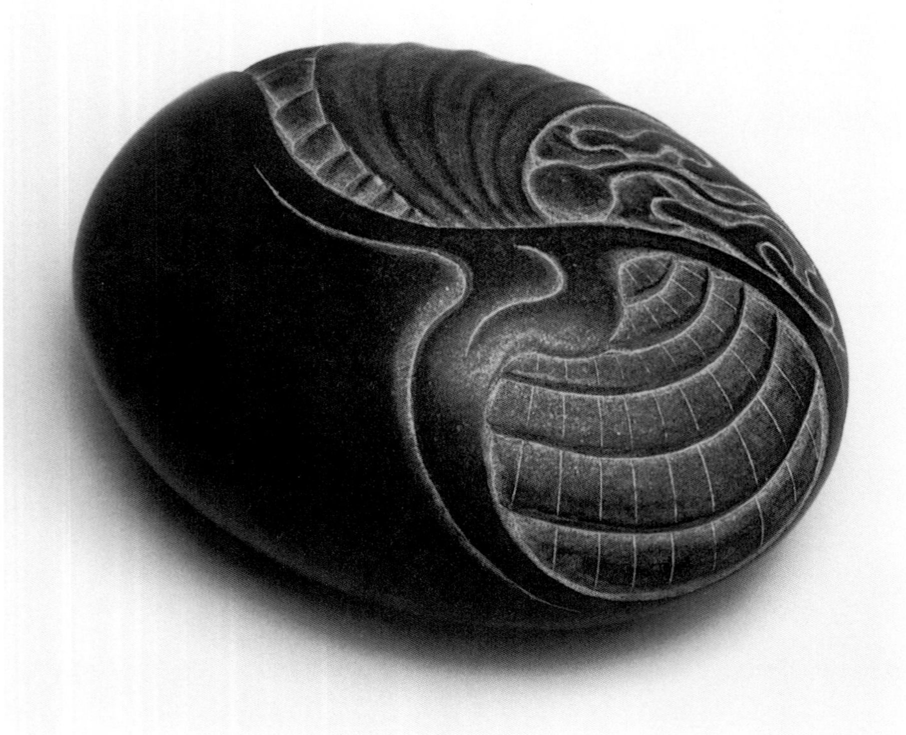

BIRTHSTONE
1998
Indian black granite
6½ x 12⅞ x 10 inches

HONORS AND AWARDS

1998 Artists Residency, The MacDowell Colony for the Arts, Peterborough, New Hampshire
1997 Al Smith Fellowship, Professional Assistance Award
1994 The Portobello Prize, London
1991 Pollock-Krasner Foundation Grant Award, New York

SELECTED SOLO EXHIBITIONS

1997 *22nd Annual Meeting*, Semiotics Society of America
1997 Icon Contemporary Art, Brunswick, Maine
1997 *Forgotten Omen*, Linda Schwartz Gallery, Lexington, Kentucky
1995 *Thomas Melville Chapin: Stone Carvings*, Reed's Wharf Gallery, London
1995 The Vrje Universiteit Brussel, Belgium

SELECTED GROUP EXHIBITIONS

1998 *1998 DeCordova Annual Exhibition*, DeCordova Museum and Sculpture Park, Lincoln, Massachusetts
1996-98 *Art for Life*, Columbus Museum of Art, Ohio
1996 Hannah Peshars Sculpture Garden, Surrey, England
1996 *Cross Currents*, The Concourse Gallery, Barbican Centre, London
1996 *Cross Currents II*, Reed's Wharf Gallery

SELECTED COLLECTIONS

- Addison Gallery of American Art, Andover, Massachusetts
- Costain Company, Lexington, Kentucky
- Jeremy Isaacs Collection, London
- Randolph-Caldwell Collection, Singapore
- University of Kentucky Art Museum, Lexington

These are some of the questions I have been thinking about recently while working:

1. What is the basic source and process of generation of dreams, visions, and hallucinations? and is it a single process?
2. How does this process(es) relate to morphic universals or archetypes (If there are such things....)
3. How does this process(es) relate to Siqueros's and Pollock's ideas of the fortuitous accident?
4. How is this different from, and in what way is it related to, luck in ordinary life?
5. What makes a person see a certain meaning in a myriad of meanings? Is this her luck?
6. How does this process differ from the subtle theory of system evolution known as self-organization? That is—is vision, dream, hallucination a natural outgrowth of sufficiently complex constituent parts at the point of phase transition (i.e. water to ice) between chaos and order?
7. In sculpture, what is this fulcrum point of phase transition between chaos and order?

To me, the most interesting elements in late 20th-century thought are the views of reality as being in a constant state of metamorphosis and symbiosis (a more Mayan than Greek idea, that is a more bio-technical and less mechanistic view). And, though my technique is very old and my imagery basic, if elusive, it is this view of reality that I try to express or at least address in my work.

BRIDGE PLAYERS, WOODFORD'S CLUB, PORTLAND
1997
c-print
30 x 36 inches

EDUCATION

1985 M.F.A., Yale University School of Art, New Haven, Connecticut
1980 B.F.A., Reed College, Portland, Oregon

HONORS AND AWARDS

1998 Alfred Eisenstadt Award, Finalist
1998 Rockefeller Study Center, Bellagio, Italy
1995 Individual Grant for Photography, New England Foundation for the Arts Fellowship
1994 John Simon Guggenheim Memorial Foundation Fellowship
1993 Individual Artists Grant, Maine Arts Commission

SELECTED SOLO EXHIBITIONS

1996 *PERSPECTIVES: Paul D'Amato*, Portland Museum of Art, Maine
1994 Museum of Contemporary Photography, Chicago
1994 Fitchburg Museum of Art, Massachusetts
1993 Northlight Gallery, Arizona State University, Tempe
1992 Photographic Resource Center, Boston

SELECTED GROUP EXHIBITIONS

1998 *11 Artists*, Photographic Resource Center
1996 *9 Artists, 9 Visions*, DeCordova Museum and Sculpture Park, Lincoln, Massachusetts
1994-95 *The Magic of Play*, Grand Central Station, New York, and the Directors Guild, Los Angeles
1993 *Wings of Change*, Directors Guild
1993 *Selections from the Permanent Collection*, Museum of Modern Art, New York

SELECTED COLLECTIONS

- Metropolitan Museum of Art, New York
- Museum of Modern Art, New York
- Rose Art Museum, Brandeis University, Waltham, Massachusetts
- Portland Museum of Art
- Museum of Contemporary Photography, Chicago

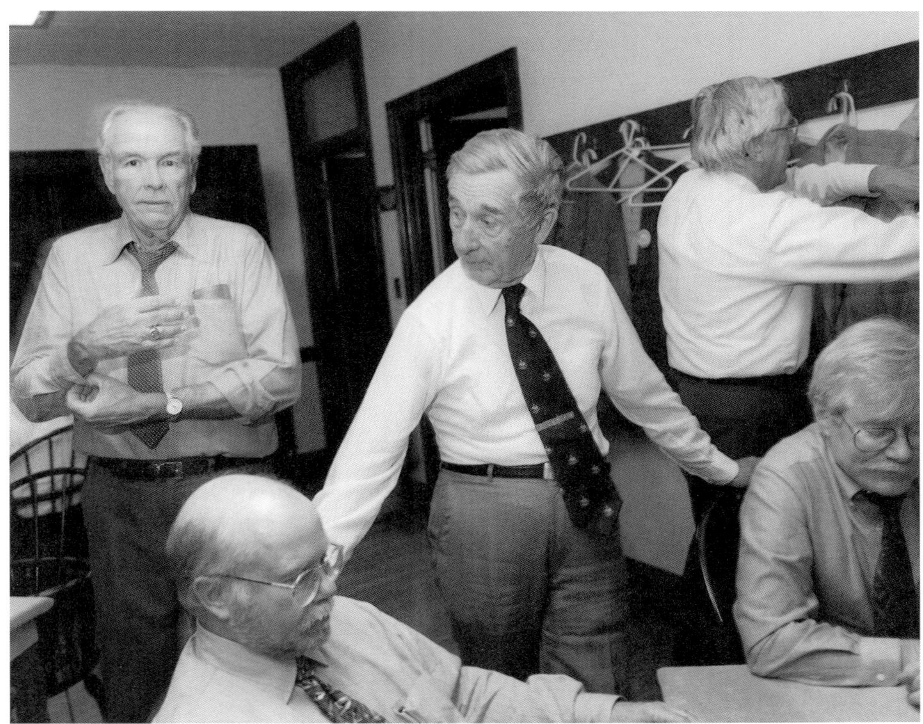

I photograph anyplace I think I can find genuine expressions of human feeling. That can be as close as the Woodford's Club in Portland or it can take me back, as it often does, to the Mexican community on the south side of Chicago. Presently, I am photographing towns along the Mexican-American border. Wherever I go, I am trying to make portraiture that negotiates the space between completely candid and partially directed.

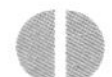 # GRACE DeGENNARO

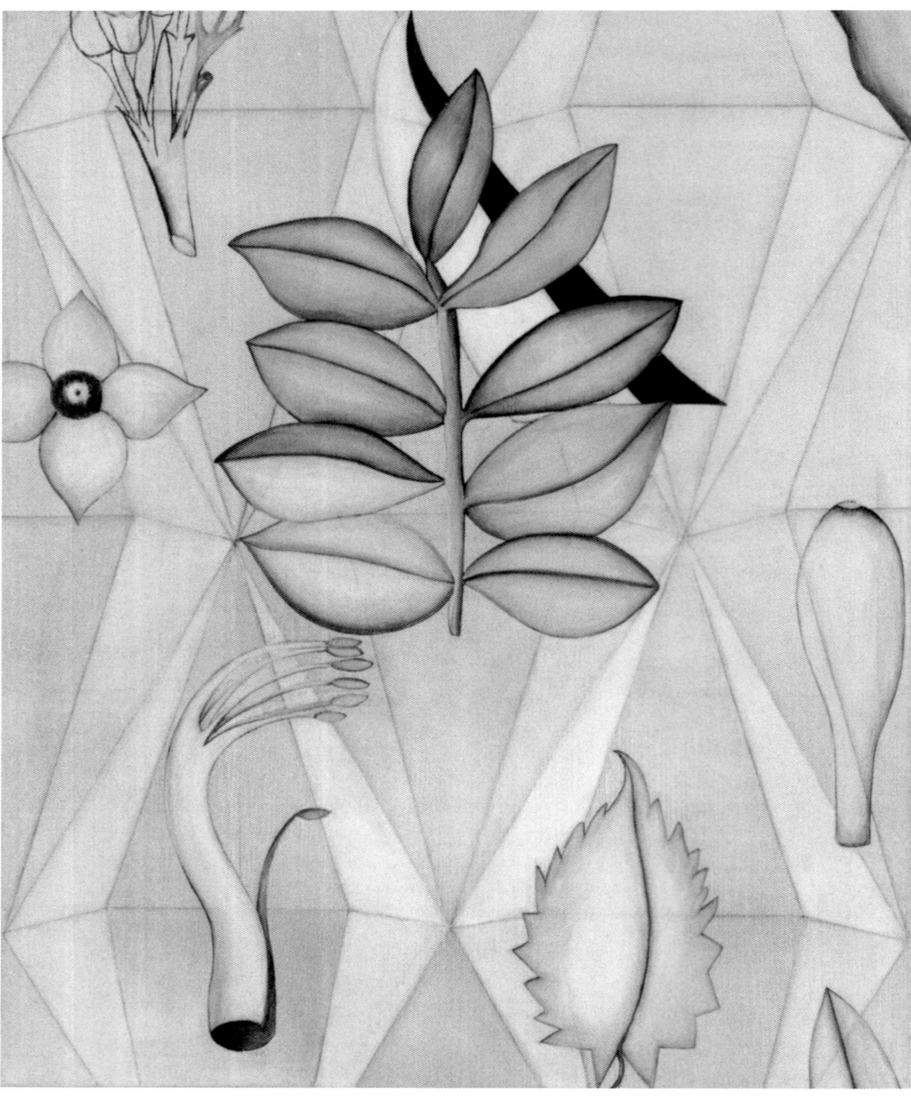

PINNATE #1
1997
oil on linen
22 x 18 x 2 inches

EDUCATION

1986   M.F.A., Painting and Sculpture, Columbia University, New York
1982-84 School of the Museum of Fine Arts, Boston
1978   B.S., Fine Arts, Skidmore College, Saratoga Springs, New York

HONORS AND AWARDS

1998   Individual Grant for works on paper, New England Foundation for the Arts Fellowship

SELECTED SOLO EXHIBITIONS

1994   *New Works*, Frick Gallery, Belfast, Maine
1994   *Tangents*, Lakes Gallery and Sculpture Garden, South Casco, Maine

SELECTED GROUP EXHIBITIONS

1997   *Works on Paper*, Clark Gallery, Lincoln, Massachusetts
1997   *Selections*, Robert Clements Gallery, Portland, Maine
1997   *4 Printmakers*, Lakes Gallery and Sculpture Garden
1997   *Three Artists*, Icon Contemporary Art, Brunswick, Maine
1997   *Images in Multiple: Six Maine Women Printmakers*, State House Gallery, Augusta, Maine

SELECTED COLLECTIONS

- Fidelity Investments
- NYNEX Corporation

I use botanical and geometric images to make work that is both abstract and realistic. Sources for my subject matter include engravings from a turn-of-the-century American dictionary and journals in which I have been recording my own dreams for 17 years. I have been working primarily with these two sources for the past four years.

The images that I have chosen to work with resonate deeply for me. I use them repeatedly. These forms and symbols suggest a myriad of references and meanings. The separate collections of images are carefully rendered, but create an open-ended narrative for the viewer. The space in my work is developed through layering. The first layer is a neutral, atmospheric color. Symmetrical images or a grid of images make the second layer. This second layer is sometimes created by projecting and drawing engravings from the dictionary onto the canvas. The images closest to the viewer are inspired by dreams. This single central image forms the third layer.

UNION RIVER BAY 7
1998
acrylic on linen
43 x 37 x 2½ inches

EDUCATION

1993 Honorary Doctorate, Fine Arts, Corcoran
Museum School of Art, Washington, DC

1952 Frank Stanton professor of Design Emeritus,
Cooper Union School for Art and
Architecture, New York

HONORS AND AWARDS

1993 Gold Medal, The American Institute of
Graphic Arts, New York

SELECTED SOLO EXHIBITIONS

1998 *Rudolph de Harak New Work*,
Icon Contemporary Art, Brunswick, Maine

1996 *Rudolph de Harak 10 year exhibition:
1986-1996 Painting and Collage*, Between
the Muse Gallery, Rockland, Maine

SELECTED GROUP EXHIBITIONS

1998 *New Acquisitions*, Farnsworth Art Museum,
Rockland, Maine

1991 *Group Show*, Judith Leighton Gallery,
Portland, Maine

SELECTED COLLECTIONS

- National Museum in Warsaw, Poland
- Farnsworth Art Museum
- Museum of Modern Art, New York
- Israel Museum, Tel Aviv

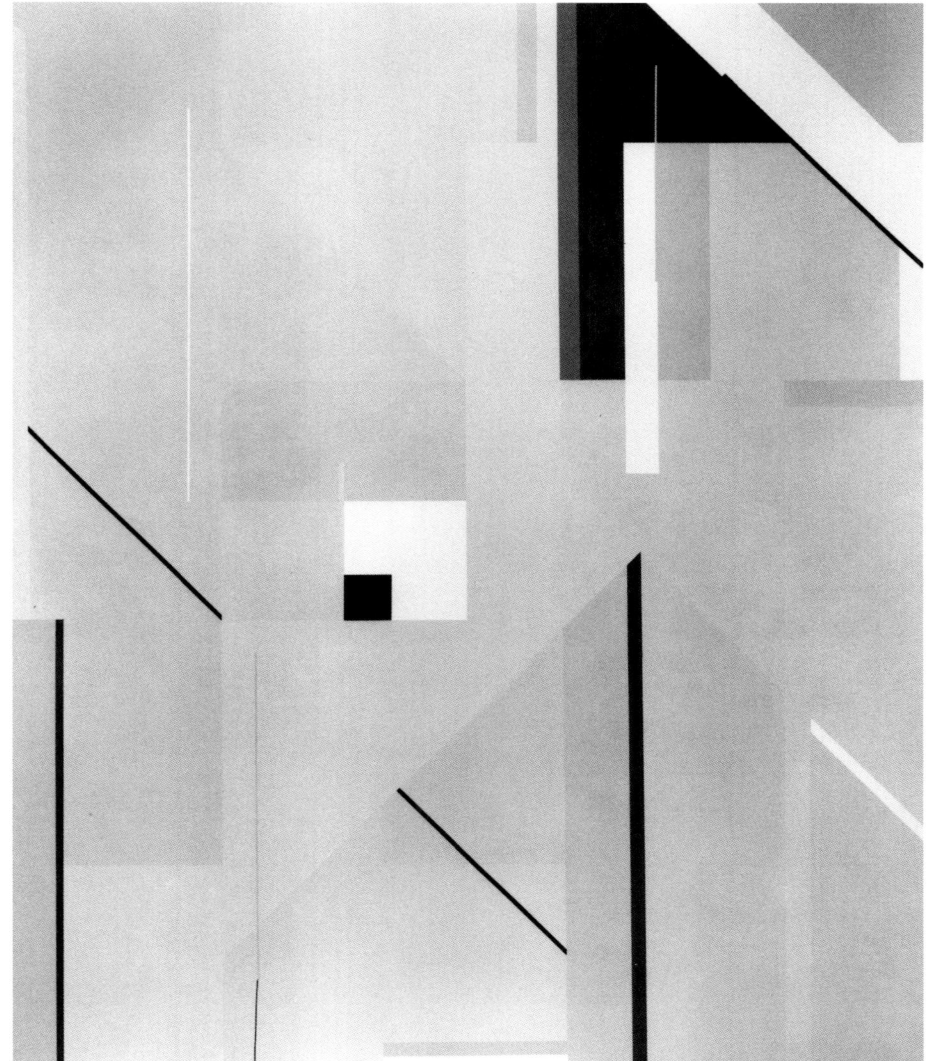

Even though my work is considered non-figurative, I don't think of myself as an abstract painter. For me, the basic geometric forms (square, circle, triangle) are quite as real as a house, a tree, or the sun and are the building blocks upon which all of our visual world is constructed. I am, however, preoccupied with clean, straight lines and hard edges. This is because I am fascinated with conspicuous visual order...and for me, this is the most efficient and rewarding way to achieve it.

What I compose is really a framework into which I can impose my feelings and expressions concerning color. What does all of this mean? Like a cloud, a wave, the sound of music or the wind, it is all very personal for each viewer and elicits different responses.

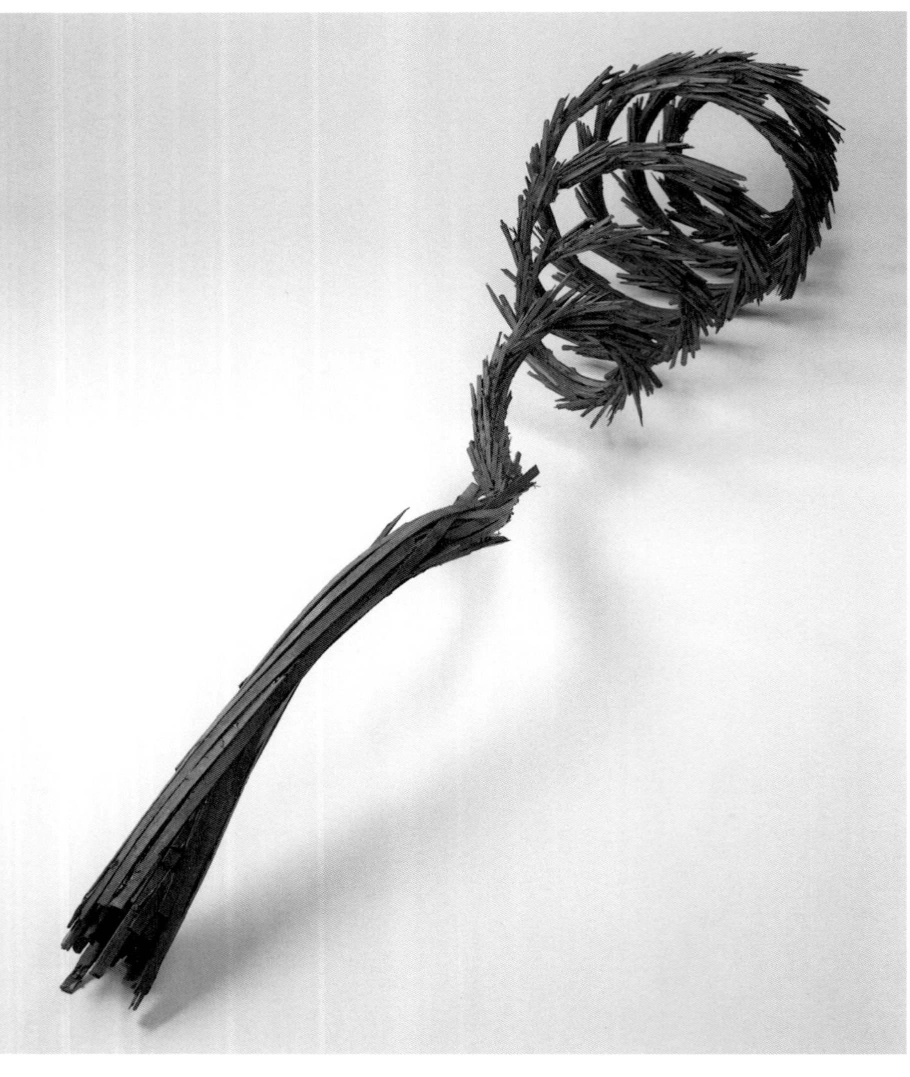

BURR
1997
cypress and mixed media
120 x 28 x 28 inches

EDUCATION

1984   B.F.A., Sculpture, University of the Arts, Philadelphia

SELECTED SOLO EXHIBITIONS

1998   Schmidt Dean Gallery, Philadelphia
1997   Between The Muse Gallery, Rockland, Maine
1995   Schmidt Dean Gallery
1995   University of the Arts
1992   Jessica Berwind Gallery, Philadelphia

SELECTED GROUP EXHIBITIONS

1998   *20 x12: A Generation of Challenged Artists*, Samuel Fleisher Art Memorial, Philadelphia
1996   *Biennial 96*, Delaware Art Museum, Wilmington
1993   *Contemporary Sculpture Directions*, Payne Gallery, Moravian College, Bethlehem, Pennsylvania
1993   *Fleisher Challenge Competition*, Samuel Fleisher Art Memorial

SELECTED COLLECTIONS

- Delaware Art Museum
- The Vanguard Group, Valley Forge, Pennsylvania
- Johnson and Johnson Company, New Brunswick, New Jersey
- American Bank, MBNA, Newark, Delaware
- Ballard, Spahr, Andrews, and Ingersoll, Philadelphia

My work is an exploration in form. I combine personal experiences with observations of natural objects found on land and under water. In constructing my sculpture I employ some of the same techniques utilized in bridge and boat construction. I bend thin strips of cypress over wood forms, often using steam to aid in the bending process. These thin strips of wood are then layered with pigmented epoxy to build a concentric form. These combinations frequently develop into symmetrical vessels or spiral structures. Grace and fluidity are achieved by using repetitive linear elements. The finishes are achieved with natural dyes and pigments suspended in lacquer varnish. The wood is frequently exposed, revealing the structural details and natural patterns and textures of the wood.

BORN: 1959, New Haven, CT

RESIDENCE: Oakland, ME

DISSEMBLING SHEATH
1997
oil on wood
12¾ x 12¾ inches

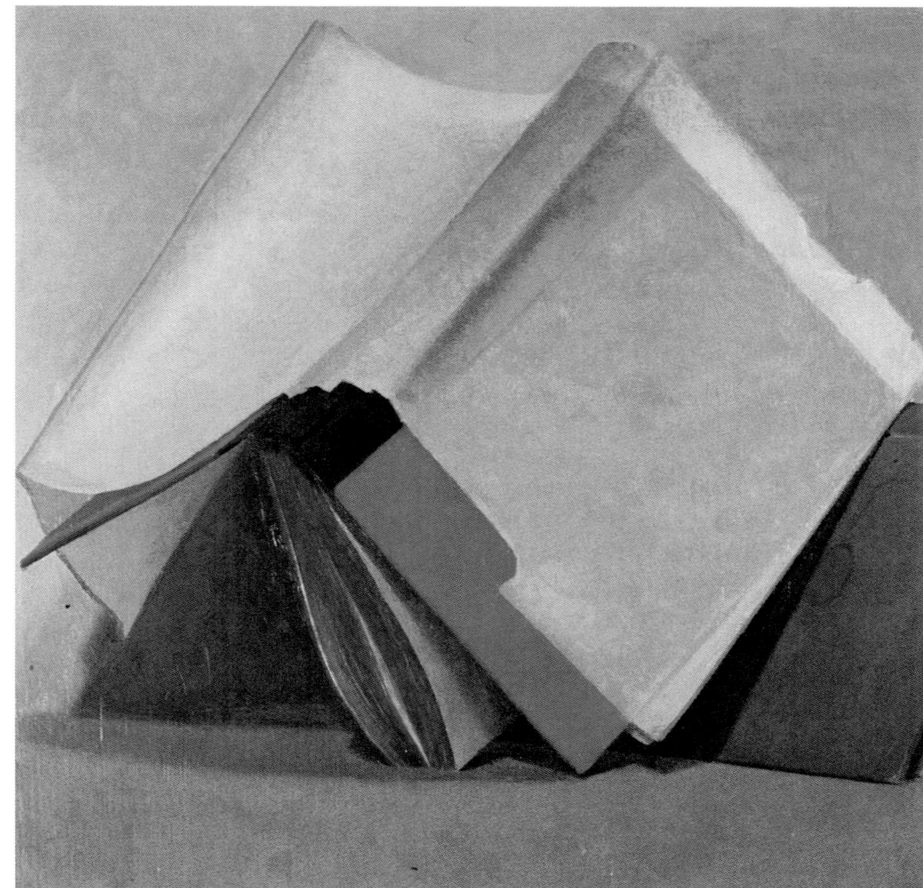

EDUCATION

1994 M.F.A., Painting, University of Pennsylvania, Philadelphia

1988 B.F.A., Portland School of Art, (now Maine College of Art)

1981 B.A., English, College of William and Mary, Williamsburg, Virginia

SELECTED SOLO EXHIBITIONS

1999 *Bevin Engman*, Colby College Museum of Art, Waterville, Maine

1998 Bachelier-Cardonsky Gallery, Kent, Connecticut

1997 Arden Gallery, Boston

1996 Bachelier-Cardonsky Gallery

1996 *Bevin Engman*, Kohn, Pedersen & Fox, New York

SELECTED GROUP EXHIBITIONS

1998 Robert Clements Gallery, Portland, Maine

1997 *The Artists' Gift*, five person show, Robert Clements Gallery

1997 *Bowery Gallery Juried Exhibition*, New York

1995 *Painting Today*, National Juried, Erector Square Gallery, New Haven, Connecticut

1995 *Women(s) Work*, National Invitational, Philadelphia

SELECTED COLLECTIONS

• Mosby Publishing, Inc., Pennsylvania

Books interest me as objects for several reasons. They have an inside and an outside with no inherent orientation. They may lie down on a side, stand firmly on one end, or balance on corners, but there is no functionally correct posture. The spine of the book serves as a rotational axis, allowing for expansion and compression of the interior volume. Because of the divisibility of the pages, the weight, torque, and balance of each book can be manipulated and redistributed. The covers may close tightly against their pages, revealing a solid block with angular planes, or they may fan open, spinning around their spine, offering ellipses and columns. It is the movement away from their initial neutral form towards a subjective use that interests me. My larger endeavor is to build a particular sense of place. For this purpose, "place" may be architectural, geographic, or psychological. Using this community of common objects, I work to convey the moment when my empirical world begins to dissolve, revealing the underlying, formal order. Associations emerge. They direct the process from the periphery of my thoughts—my childhood search for unique spaces in which to play, the quality of light and air in locations I have lived, the nature of human relationships. Although these associations spring from my experience, I am not seeking to provide overt personal narratives. I seek instead a formal language of remembrances which evoke feelings of intense familiarity, and, in some cases, longing.

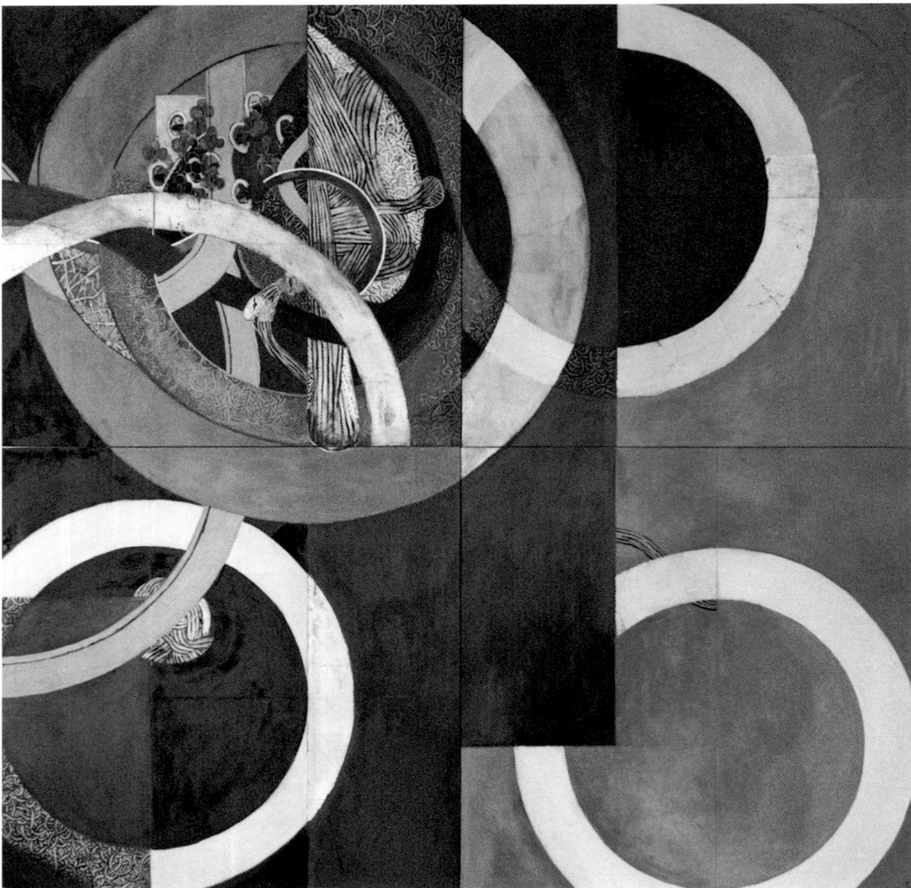

VOICE
1997
oil and metal leaf on wood
72 x 72 inches

EDUCATION
1989   Maine-Dartmouth Family Practice Residency, Augusta
1986   M.D., Mt. Sinai School of Medicine, New York
1984   Skowhegan School of Painting and Sculpture, Maine
1980   B.A., Physics, Dartmouth College, Hanover, New Hampshire

HONORS AND AWARDS
1993   Artists Residency, The MacDowell Colony for the Arts, Peterborough, New Hampshire

SELECTED SOLO EXHIBITIONS
1997   *Sexual Water*, Caldbeck Gallery, Rockland, Maine
1995   *Internal Affairs*, Caldbeck Gallery
1992   *Meditations on Loss*, Chocolate Church, Bath, Maine

SELECTED GROUP EXHIBITIONS
1996   *Skowhegan at 50: The Maine Legacy*, Maine Coast Artists, Rockport
1995   *Winter's Work*, Frick Gallery, Belfast, Maine
1995   *Moments*, Ellsworth Library Gallery, Maine
1993   *What's Going on Now?—A Democratic Survey of New Art in Maine*, Frick Gallery
1992   *Group Show*, Frick Gallery

These paintings are from a series which strives to provoke a dialogue on the spiritual and scientific notions of unity and differentiation. Many of the paintings incorporate layers of information. Specific references are made to embryology, the differentiation of singular fetal genitals into male and female forms, the manual assessment of pregnancy, and the scientific representation of partial blindness. These diagrams are incorporated into map-like structures which refer to both the human body and art traditions created for facilitating visualization, such as Jain cosmological maps and Tibetan mandalas.

The paintings are on wood, including plywood and doors. The surfaces are, in places, shallowly carved and scarred. These are mixed media pieces which include Xerox transfers from texts, oil paint, and gold and metal leaf.

THE TARR AND WONSON COPPER PAINT MANUFACTORY
1997
seven color reduction woodcut on Okawara paper
34 x 26 inches

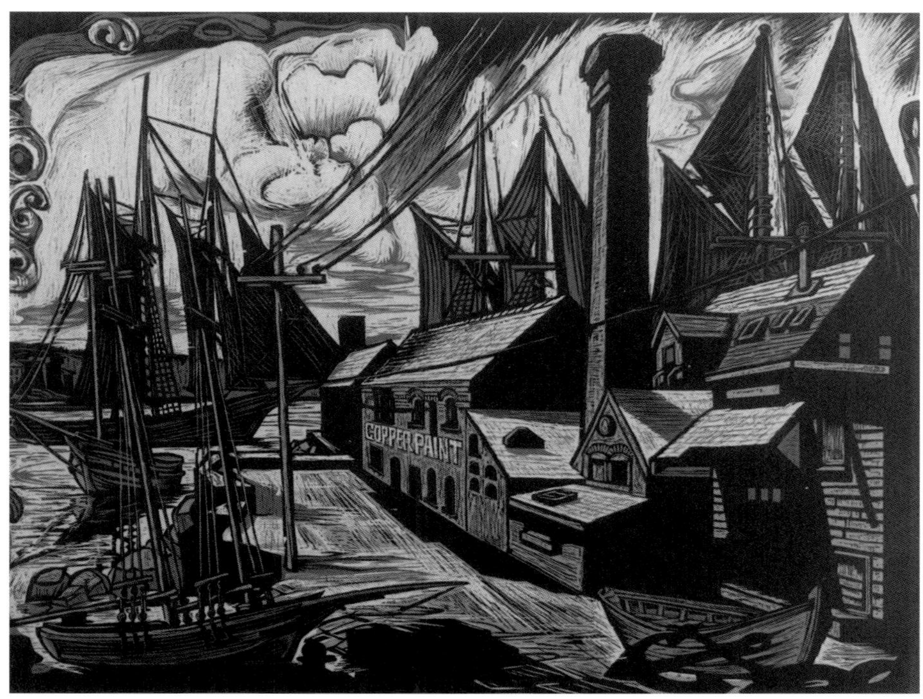

EDUCATION

1972　School of the Museum of Fine Arts, Boston

HONORS AND AWARDS

1968　Ford Fellowship to School of the Museum of
Fine Arts, Boston

SELECTED SOLO EXHIBITIONS

1998　*Working Waterfronts from Provincetown
to Portland,* Wholfarth Galleries,
Provincetown, Massachusetts
1995　*A City at River's Edge,* Point Gallery,
Harbour Place, Portsmouth, New Hampshire
1992　*Woodcuts of the Northshore,* Wintisky
Gallery, Salem State College, Massachusetts

SELECTED GROUP EXHIBITIONS

1996　*National Print Biennial,* Silvermine Guild
Arts Center, New Canaan, Connecticut
1995　*Maine Printmaking,* Round Top Center for
the Arts, Damariscotta, Maine
1994　*Woodcuts and Drawings,* Maine Coast
Artists, Rockport
1994　*Architecture in Contemporary Printing,*
Boston Printmakers Traveling Show
1993　*Mainescapes 1900-1992,* Ogunquit Museum
of American Art, Maine

SELECTED COLLECTIONS

- Portland Museum of Art, Maine
- United Litho Co., Somerville, Massachusetts
- Cape Ann Historical Museum, Gloucester,
Massachusetts
- United Technologies, Hartford, Connecticut
- Ogunquit Museum of American Art

These woodcuts express the abstract geometric shapes and distant configurations of architecture in the Northeast. Upon the sea waters of estuaries and harbors are mirrored the play of interweaving light and dark of the buildings and piers crowned by steeples and mast tops. I am fascinated by the ghostly quality of these buildings looming out of the mist, endowed with strength and endurance. For me, historic architecture represents a bridge from one lifespan into another. Abandoned not by time, but by those who build them, our structures remain and continue to wage war with nature's elements.

ERIC GREEN

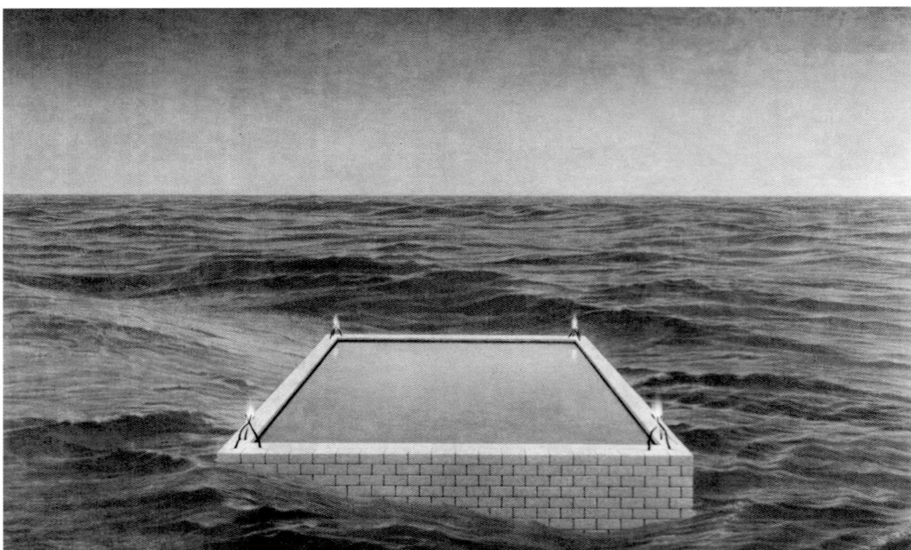

POOL
1996
oil on canvas
40 x 65 inches

HONORS AND AWARDS

1996   Merit Award, National Academy of Design,
New York

SELECTED SOLO EXHIBITIONS

1997   Gallery Henoch, New York

SELECTED GROUP EXHIBITIONS

1997   *Realism in 20th-Century American Painting*,
Ogunquit Museum of American Art,
Maine
1995-97 *Art from the Driver's Seat: Americans and
their Cars*, Traveling Show, 10 regional
museums
1996   *171st Annual Exhibition*, National Academy
of Design
1996   *Fall Group Show*, Gallery Henoch
1993   *Mainescapes: 1900-1992*, Ogunquit
Museum of American Art

SELECTED COLLECTIONS

• Portland Museum of Art, Maine

OVER BLUE
1998
acrylic on canvas
28 x 28 inches

EDUCATION

1968 Graduate Studies, Assumption College, Worcester, Massachusetts

1967 B.F.A., Painting and Graphics, University of New Hampshire, Durham

SELECTED SOLO EXHIBITIONS

1996 One Person Show, Icon Contemporary Art, Brunswick, Maine

SELECTED GROUP EXHIBITIONS

1998 *Abstraction x 3: Paintings by Jessyca Broekman, Martha Groome, and Brigitte Keller*, Ogunquit Museum of American Art, Maine

1998 Two-Person Show, Icon Contemporary Art

1997 *Accord II,* Old York Historical Society, York, Maine

1995 *Mainescapes: Women Artists, 1900-1995,* Ogunquit Museum of American Art

I ask how it is, what it is, why it is about everything, all the time. I approach painting in terms of such questions, and I have answered them by reducing the number of elements that I use in a painting so that its nature might become true and clear. Having first sorted the clues of appearances, I put aside anything unessential, distracting, or irrelevant in order to see the problem in front of me. I believe that, at the point of near-nothing, the unknown and the new become obvious. My intention is to make a sensation of presence with no instructions.

TOM HALL

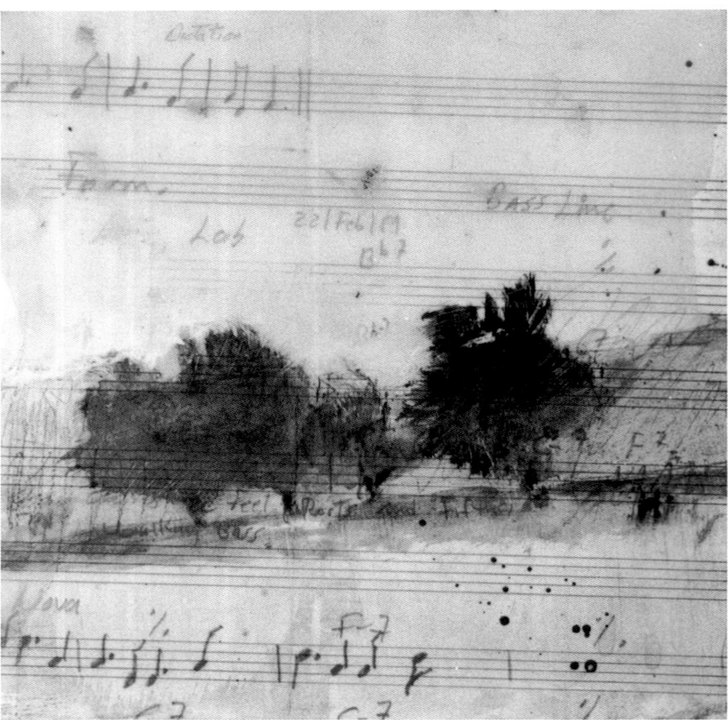

McAULEY ORCHARD
1996
mixed media on paper
6 x 6 x 1½ inches

EDUCATION
1979   University of Oregon, Eugene

SELECTED SOLO EXHIBITIONS
1999   O'Farrell Gallery, Brunswick, Maine
1997   University of Southern Maine Art Gallery, Gorham
1997   Bromfield Gallery, Boston
1996   O'Farrell Gallery
1994   Greenhut Gallery, Portland, Maine

SELECTED GROUP EXHIBITIONS
1998   *Annual Juried Exhibition*, Maine Coast Artists, Rockport
1998   *Peregrine Press Printmaking at MCA*, Maine Coast Artists
1996   *Members Show*, O'Farrell Gallery
1995   *Attleboro Forum 95*, Attleboro Museum, Massachusetts
1995   *17th Annual Juried Show*, Maine Coast Artists

SELECTED COLLECTIONS
- *The Boston Globe*
- The Prudential Life Insurance Company, Boston
- Portland Museum of Art, Maine

I love landscapes.

It probably has something to do with this autumn scratch of branches against the house...something about this housebound October mope. Desk sat, with the clutter of life before me...I wonder if it might well be an "age" thing...this bias toward the landscape. Man's forever preoccupation with "new," and with "change," just doesn't seem to interest me anymore...or at least as much as it used to. More and more the paintings want to be, contrarily, an anchor first...and then an instigator.

And, I love the Landscape.

It's a "beauty" thing also...this back door passion with the landscape. And though beauty can, indeed, be just another opiate...somehow today (as this afternoon light ebbs across my feet), it seems a much needed balm for this bird feeder frenzy in my soul. In the beauty is a silence...made up of the likes of Inness, of Cather, and of great timeless architecture like Richardson's Trinity Church. And into this soup of silence, on any given day, I'll toss a DeKooning, H.V. Miller...maybe a Leonard Cohen tune and, usually against my wishes, yesterday's news. Trying to layer the "opiate" with consequences...so that just maybe...beauty can aspire to Beauty.

Both, I find to be great antidotes to man.

In my mind I hear an early flock of October geese, tucked down behind foliaged trees...sort of a sing song tirade, a melancholic forecast for this fleeting by Fall. And like the palm of a hand, I sense the day/the season closing preciously about me...calling me out. Instigated...(with hat in one hand and pastels in the other)...silly me with great American painting in mind...I'm door slammed, porch crossed, and off into the fields...

BORN: 1962, Walla Walla, WA

RESIDENCE: Freeport, ME

FLIGHT VI
1996
gelatin silver print
20 x 16 inches

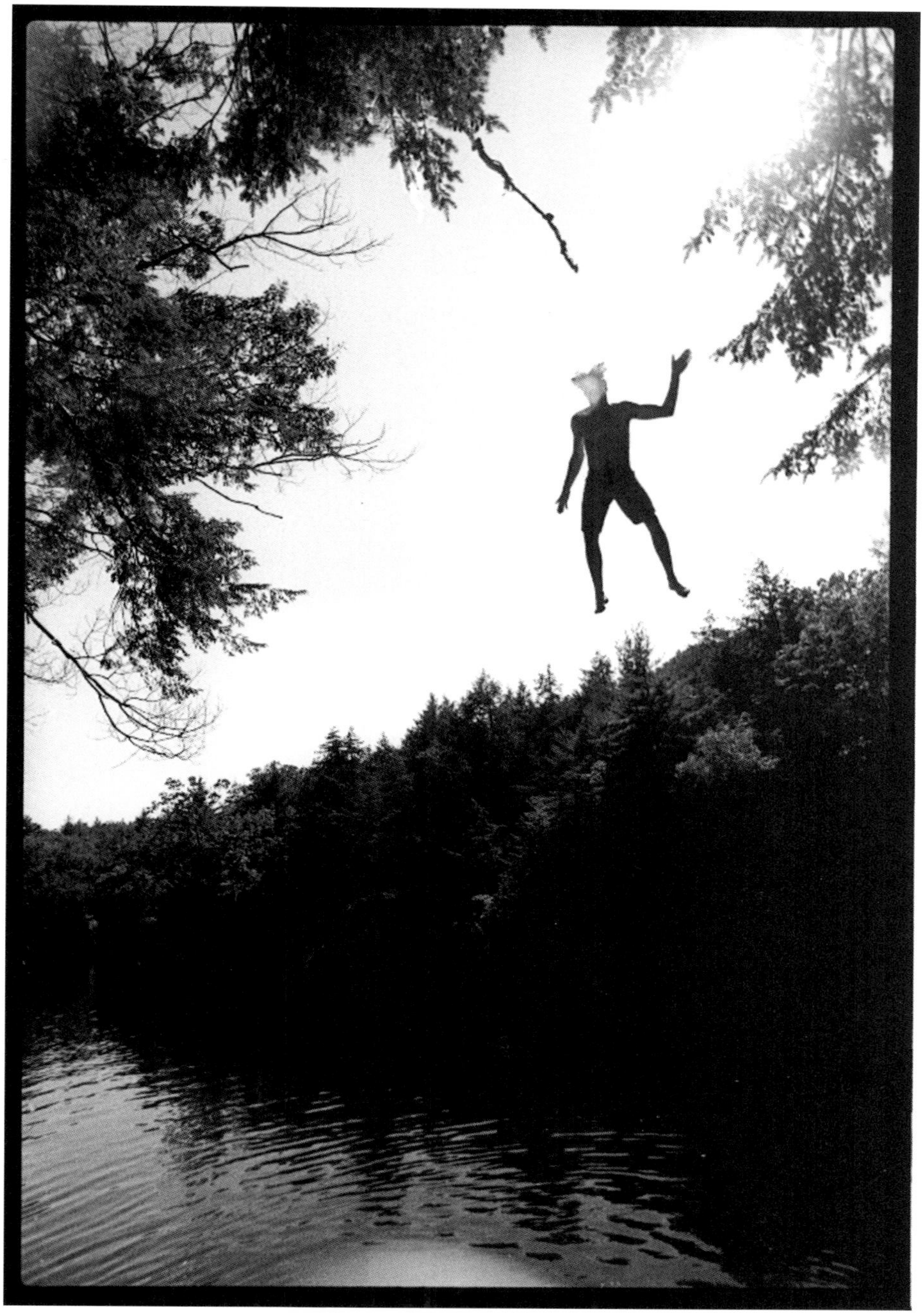

EDUCATION
1986   B.S.J., Visual Communications, Ohio
University, Athens

SELECTED SOLO EXHIBITIONS
1994   *Elmer Walker: Hermit to Hero*, Maine Coast
Artists, Rockport (shown 1998 at the Institute
of Contemporary Art, Maine College of
Art, Portland)
1994   *Maine Musicians*, Portland Performing Arts
Center

SELECTED GROUP EXHIBITIONS
1995   *Maine, A Peopled Landscape: Salt
Documentary Photography, 1978-1995*,
Portland Museum of Art, Maine
1995   *Artistic Nourishment*, Maine Artist
Fellowship winners, Bath, Maine
1992-94 *New England Photographers*, Danforth
Museum of Art, Framingham, Massachusetts

SELECTED COLLECTIONS
- Portland Museum of Art
- Danforth Museum of Art

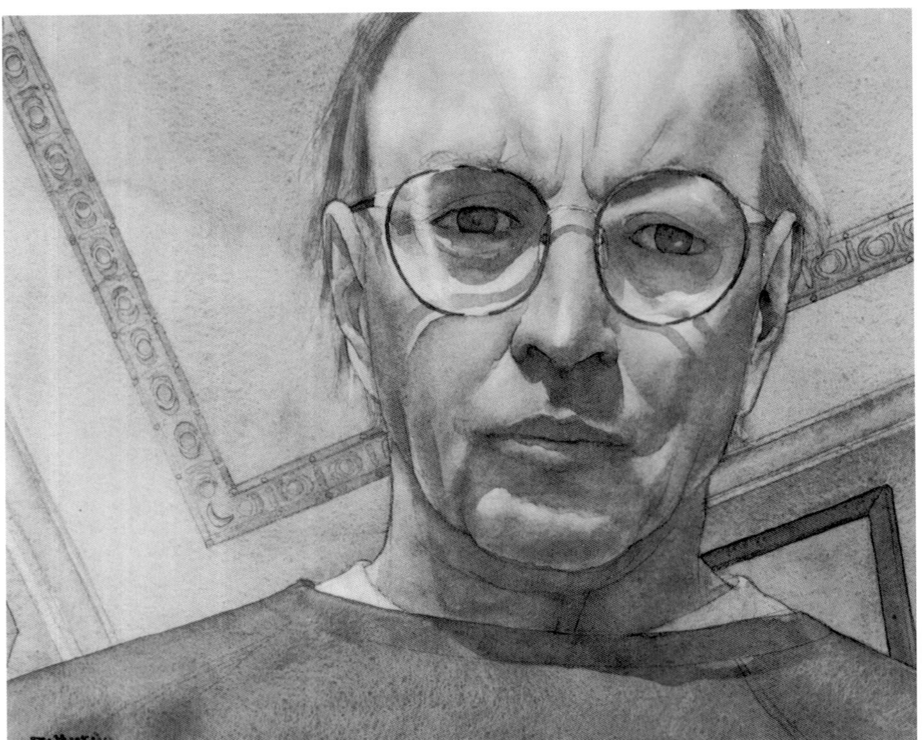

SELF PORTRAIT
1998
watercolor on paper
12 x 18 inches

SELECTED GROUP EXHIBITIONS

1992 *On the Edge: Forty Years of Maine Painting 1952-1992*, Maine Coast Artists, Rockport

SELECTED COLLECTIONS

- The Fine Arts Museums of San Francisco, M.H. DeYoung Memorial Museum
- Smithsonian Institution, Washington, DC
- Library of Congress, Washington, DC
- The British Museum, London

SECOND PORTRAIT WITH MAX
1996-97
oil on canvas
46 x 30 inches

EDUCATION

1988 M.F.A., Yale University School of Art, New Haven, Connecticut

1986 B.F.A., Washington University, St. Louis, Missouri

HONORS AND AWARDS

1998 Artist-in-Residency Grant, Roswell, New Mexico

1997 John Simon Guggenheim Memorial Foundation Fellowship

1993 National Endowment for the Arts Visual Artists Fellowship

1993 Volglestein Foundation Grant

SELECTED SOLO EXHIBITIONS

1998 Roswell Museum of Art, New Mexico

1997 Nielsen Gallery, Boston

1997 Maine Coast Artists, Rockport

1994 Nielsen Gallery

1993 Emmanuel College, Boston

SELECTED GROUP EXHIBITIONS

1998 *Knowing Children*, David Beitzel Gallery, New York

1998 *Group Show*, Tatistcheff Gallery, New York

1997 *Eleven Faces*, The Painting Center, New York

1996 *9 Artists, 9 Visions*, DeCordova Museum and Sculpture Park, Lincoln, Massachusetts

1996 *Narcissism: Artists Reflect Themselves*, California Center for the Arts Museum, Escondido

SELECTED COLLECTIONS

- Boston Public Library
- Bowdoin College Museum of Art, Brunswick, Maine
- DeCordova Museum and Sculpture Park
- Olin Arts Center, Bates College, Lewiston, Maine
- Yale University Art Gallery

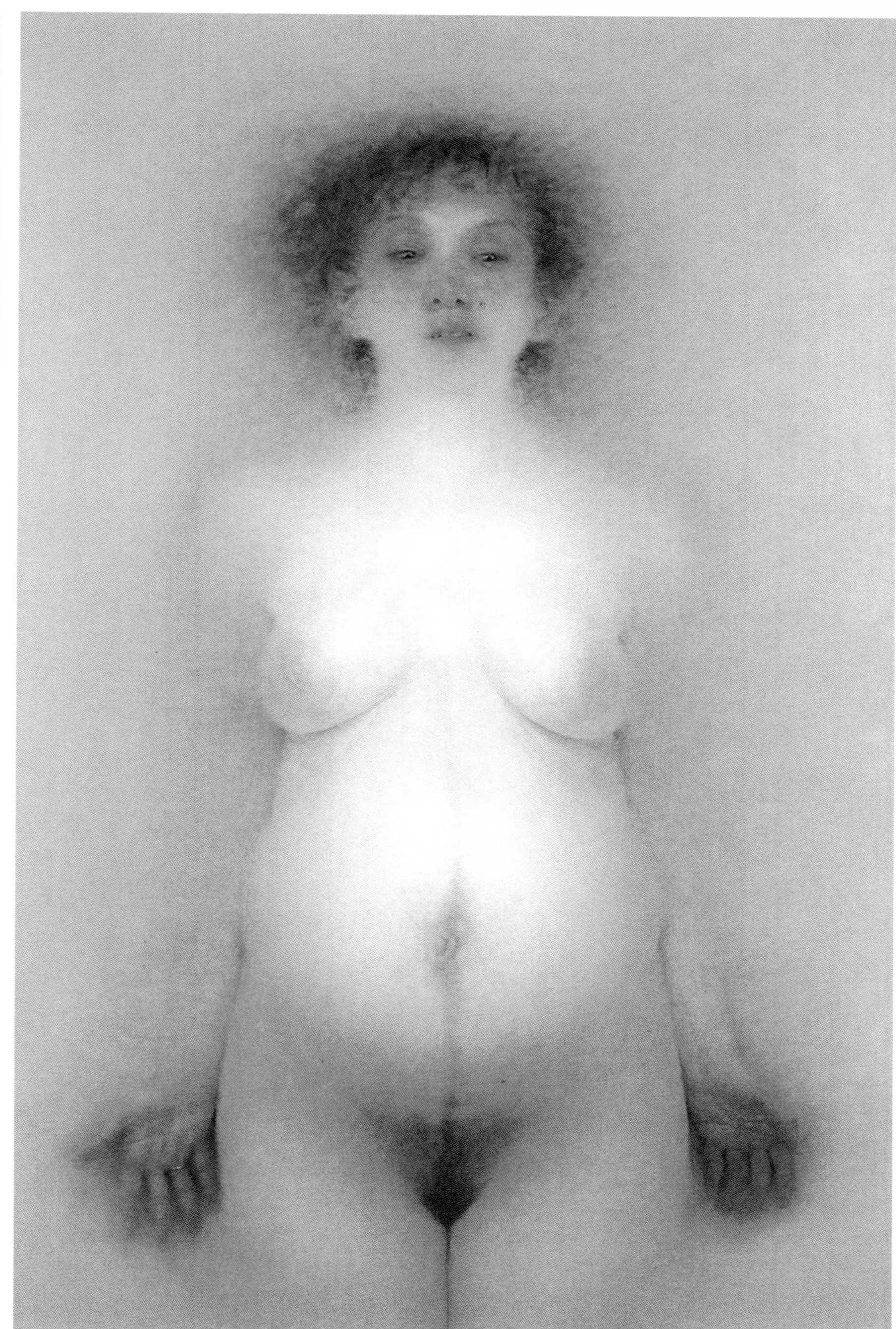

Here are some things other people have said that I think about a lot.

"Spirituality is the foundation of art." Alice Walker

"God is in the details." Mies van der Rohe

"Any life provides enough to fuel an entire career." John Updike

"Emotion is a feeling, not a style." Richard Thompson

DANIEL HEYMAN

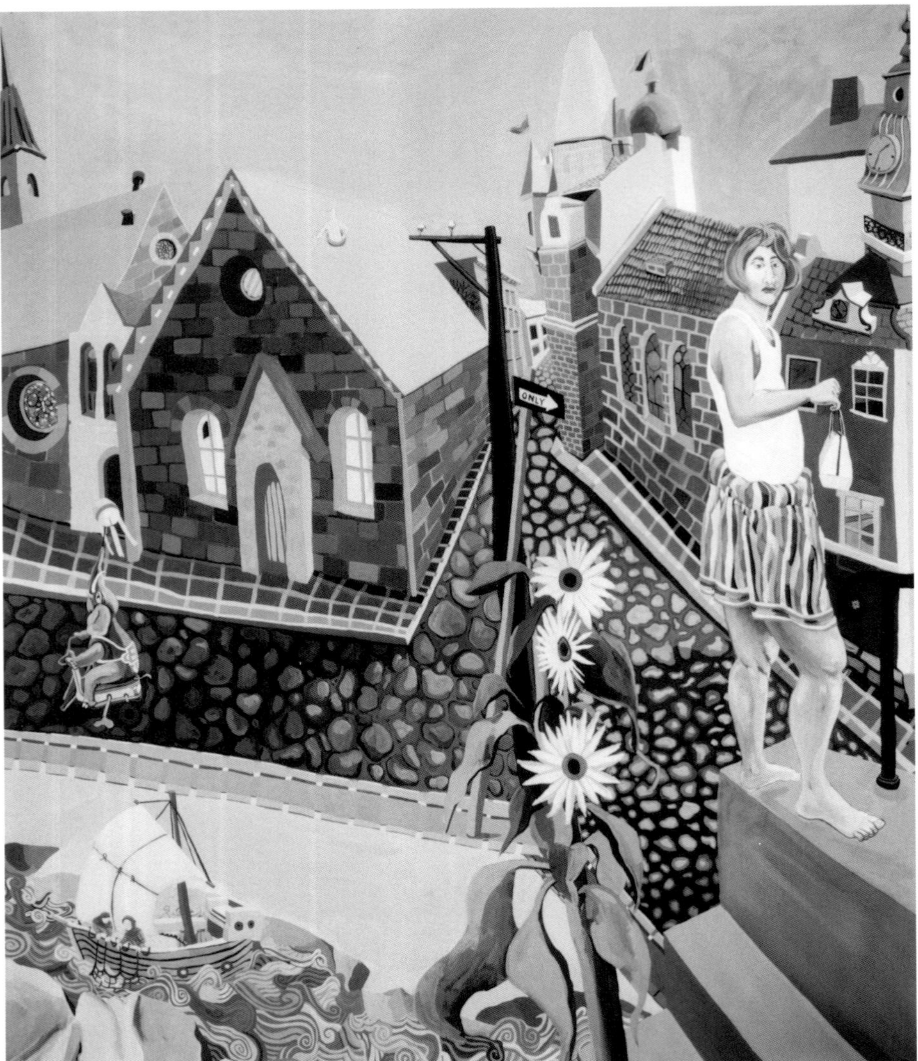

ON THE WAY TO FRED'S
1998
gouache on paper
54 x 45 inches

EDUCATION

1991   M.F.A., University of Pennsylvania, Philadelphia

1985   A.B., Dartmouth College, Hanover, New Hampshire

HONORS AND AWARDS

1994   Forest Fellow, Millay Colony for the Arts, Austerlitz, New York

SELECTED SOLO EXHIBITIONS

1998   55 Mercer Street Gallery, New York

1997   Mangel Gallery, Philadelphia

1995   Morgan Print Gallery, Philadelphia

1994   Gallery B.A.I., New York

1994   Dolan/Maxwell Gallery, Philadelphia

SELECTED GROUP EXHIBITIONS

1998   Long Beach Museum of Art, California

1998   Broadway Gallery, Troy, New York

1997   William Way Community Center, Philadelphia

1997   Paley Gallery, Philadelphia College of Textiles and Science, Faculty Show

1997   Community Art Center, Faculty Show, Wallingford, Pennsylvania

I have always been interested in painting as a vehicle for narrative and political content. In 1986, I received a Reynolds Fellowship from Dartmouth College to collect very personal memories of World War II through individual interviews. I used those memories for my first series of narrative paintings. I have never been concerned with form for its own sake, nor have I bothered to make art about art. Personally, I find this approach too narrow. I want my work to resonate with people entirely unengaged with the arts, as well as with those intimately associated with contemporary art issues. I paint almost always in gouache, combining stories from many different sources, leading the viewer to make connections among different kinds of events and thoughts. I also make ceramic mosaics, quilts, and textile pieces.

ATTEMPT 1
1997
oil and wax on masonite
36 x 36 inches

EDUCATION

1997   M.F.A., Painting and Drawing, School of The Art Institute of Chicago, Illinois

1996   Skowhegan School of Painting and Sculpture, Maine

1989   B.F.A., Painting and Drawing, School of The Art Institute of Chicago

SELECTED GROUP EXHIBITIONS

1997   *Two Person Show*, Contemporary Art Workshop, Chicago

1997   *New Talent I*, Contemporary Art Workshop

1997   *M.F.A. Show*, School of The Art Institute of Chicago

1996   *Young Americans of Asian Ancestry*, Hyde Park Art Center, Chicago

1996   *Juried Group Show*, Gallery 2, Chicago

My paintings convey the conflicts and contradictions I have within myself. I am propelled to feel the accidental, meaningless, and unpurposed nature of being. However, I am emphatic that I do exist every day and I am unable to admit one's being as nothing. I am trying to capture these inescapable and helpless feelings by depicting the specific psychological state and situation. Recently, I have been using images of figures trying to be unseen, trying to become part of the landscape, trying to withdraw themselves, and trying to treat themselves and their time as unimportant. However, the figures are not quite succeeding in such attempts.

Although it is essential that my paintings stay true and close to myself without any compromise or adjustment made for others, I am hoping, at the same time, that they will communicate to some viewers who share a similar feeling.

SHERRILL EDWARDS HUNNIBELL

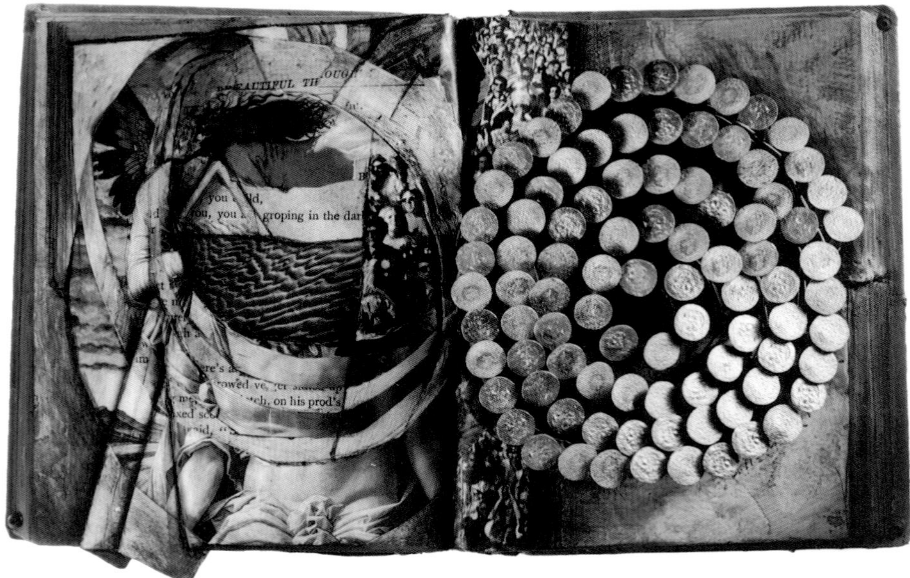

**BOOK OF HOURS #44:
GROPING IN THE DARK**
1996
mixed media altered book
6 x 9¼ x 1¼ inches

Historically, the "Book of Hours" was a small, hand-held day-book used primarily by women and the clergy for guidance in meditation. Working in my studio, I find a personal form of meditation through the manipulation of surfaces and shifts in visual relationships.

Each piece in the *Book of Hours* series, which now numbers over 50 works, is constructed from an actual book—one chosen for its physical potential rather than its literary content. The altered books and other works are influenced by my affection for maps, books, and hand-woven and knotted structures such as baskets and prayer rugs—all of which I see as being containers or communicators of the physical and spiritual and as sharing common ground through the interaction of the human hand.

My work deals with themes familiar to most artists: mysteries and memories, transitions and transformations, balances between science/technology and nature/mythology, and relationships between the *container* and the *contained*.

EDUCATION

1966 M.A.T., Brown University, Providence, Rhode Island

1964 B.F.A., Rhode Island School of Design, Providence

HONORS AND AWARDS

1998 Residency Fellowships, Leighton Studios, The Banff Centre for the Arts, Alberta, Canada (also 1994, 1992, and 1991)

1994 Fellowship, Virginia Center for the Creative Arts, Sweet Briar

SELECTED SOLO EXHIBITIONS

1998 *Altered Books and Works-On-Paper*, Providence Athenaeum, Rhode Island

1997 *Altered Books, Showcase Exhibition*, Milwaukee Institute of Art and Design, Wisconsin

1994 *Unexpected Journeys: Part II*, Trustman Gallery, Simmons College, Boston

1993 *Unexpected Journeys: Part I*, Dodge House Gallery, Providence

1992 *Book of Hours*, Sarah Doyle Gallery, Brown University

SELECTED GROUP EXHIBITIONS

1998 *Invitational: Four Artists*, Gallery House, Nobleboro, Maine

1998 *The Painted Word*, Sarah Doyle Gallery

1997 *Grammar of Collage IV*, HERA Gallery, Wakefield, Rhode Island

1996 *Grammar of Collage II*, Dodge House Gallery

1995 *Contemporary Collage and Assemblage*, Frick Gallery, Belfast, Maine

SELECTED COLLECTIONS

- The Banff Centre for the Arts, Artists' Book Collection
- The Prudential Collection, Newark, New Jersey
- DeCordova Museum and Sculpture Park, Lincoln, Massachusetts
- The First National Bank of Boston Collection
- The Edmund Mauro Collection, Providence

THE FOREST
1997-98
mixed media on wood
84 x variable x ¾ inches

EDUCATION

1950   B.F.A., Painting, Yale University School of Art, New Haven, Connecticut

HONORS AND AWARDS

1997   The ASW Award (Major Award for Painting), Art of the Northeast USA, Silvermine Guild Arts Center, New Canaan, Connecticut

1992   Individual Grant for Painting, New England Foundation for the Arts/National Endowment for the Arts

SELECTED SOLO EXHIBITIONS

1998   Richmond Art Center, Loomis Chaffee School, Windsor, Connecticut

1993   *Connections: An Exhibition of Two Friends*, Silvermine Guild Arts Center

1993   *A Ten Year Retrospective*, Hurlbutt Gallery, Friends of the Greenwich Library, Connecticut

SELECTED GROUP EXHIBITIONS

1998   *Connecticut Women Artists*, New Britain Museum of American Art

1997   *Studio Work*, Between The Muse Gallery, Rockland, Maine

1997   *Art of the Northeast USA*, Silvermine Guild Arts Center

1997   *Monotype Quartet*, The Drawing Room Gallery, St. George, Maine

1996   *Foreword*, SOHO 20, New York

SELECTED COLLECTIONS

- Xerox Corporation, Greenwich, Connecticut
- General Electric Company, Fairfield, Connecticut
- Marketing Corporation of America, Westport, Connecticut
- Town of Fairfield Collection, Connecticut
- Aaron Green Associates, New York

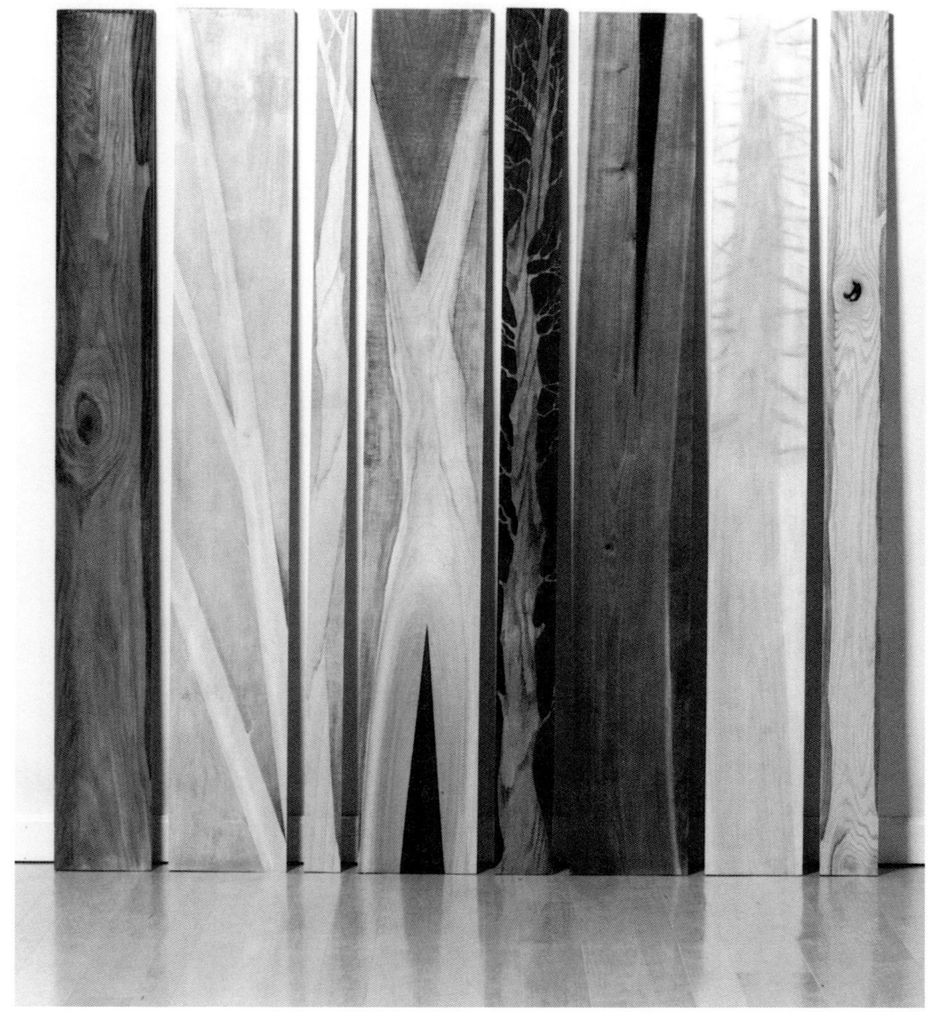

The focus of my art-making for the past several years has been the exploration of the properties of wood in two-dimensional work. While using different types of plywood and laminations, coupled with various painting techniques, I realized that the wood was becoming an integral part of the art, and not just a working surface.

In consequence, though the nature of the wood had always been important, it was now the grain of the wood that was central. Thus, I began to spend much time searching for "guiding grains" in the hardwood section of The Home Depot. During this process, the inherent logic of a tree image with its own defining structure, placed on its own hardwood plank, following its own grain became evident; the idea of an installation, *The Forest*, an atmosphere of the essence of trees, was born.

At present, this consists of 52 planks, all the same height, of varying widths, each with a different tree image. The very limitation of size, shape, surface, and grain works as a creative tool.

EUGENE KOCH

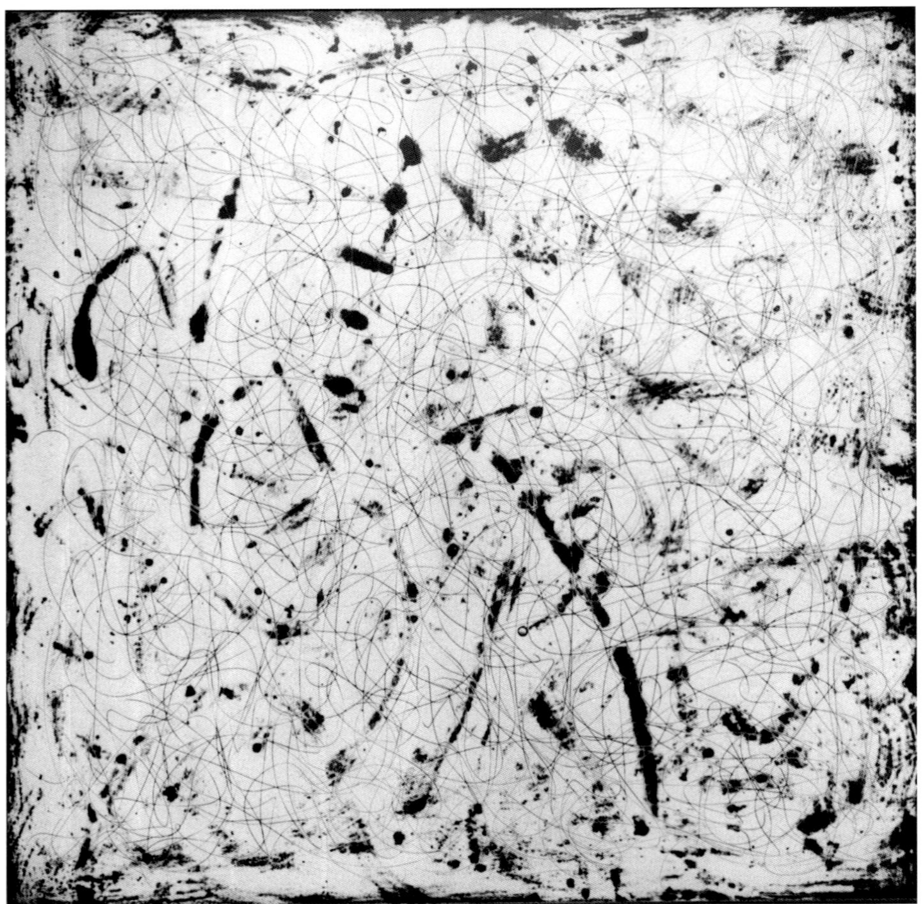

SEA SMOKE #15
1997
India ink on clayboard
24 x 24 inches

EDUCATION
1973   B.A., Tufts University, Medford,
        Massachusetts

SELECTED SOLO EXHIBITIONS
1997   *Beneath the Surface*, Visual Art Gallery,
        Boston
1997   *Recent Paintings*, Davidson & Daughters
        Contemporary Art, Portland, Maine
1996   *Loveseat Blues*, June Fitzpatrick Gallery,
        Portland, Maine
1996   *Recent Clayboards*, Deer Isle Artists
        Association, Maine

SELECTED GROUP EXHIBITIONS
1998   *Annual Juried Exhibition*, Maine Coast
        Artists, Rockport
1996   *Interiors*, Union of Maine Visual Artists,
        Mount Desert
1995   *Annual Juried Exhibition*, Maine Coast Artists
1993   *From Floor to Ceiling*, University of Southern
        Maine, Gorham
1993   *Annual Juried Exhibition*, Maine Coast Artists

The *Sea Smoke* series of paintings were made in the past year and are a continuation of work I've made since 1994. For those of you not near these northern shores in winter—sea smoke is the mist rising off the sea when the air is around zero degrees or less—it can be quite wonderful and beautiful, especially off Stonington in an early morning light with the dark islands appearing now and then through the sea smoke streaming off the water. That combination of energy and contemplative vision is what I strive for in my own work, and the black ink forms appearing through the white surface remind me of this numinous phenomenon, and hence, the name of the series.

CLEARING
1997
turpentine wash on paper
28 x 38 inches

EDUCATION

1975   M.F.A., Painting, State University College, New Paltz, New York

1964   M.A., Painting, Michigan State University, East Lansing

1963   B.S., Art Education, State University College

SELECTED SOLO EXHIBITIONS

1997   *Entrance Into Mystery: The Maine Landscape*, Uptown Gallery, New York

1996   *Place By the River*, Gallery 210, University of Missouri, St. Louis

1995   *Celebration of Light: The Maine Landscape*, Uptown Gallery

1995   *Magic is Alive*, University of Maine Museum of Art, Orono

1994   New England Foundation for the Arts, Cambridge, Massachusetts

SELECTED GROUP EXHIBITIONS

1998   *Painterly Bravura*, Steven Scott Gallery, Baltimore, Maryland

1998   *Radiant Passage*, Gallery 357 Main, Rockland, Maine

1997   *Recent Acquisitions*, Portland Museum of Art, Maine

1993   *Collecting for Harvard: Work Acquired through the Generosity of Melvin R. Seiden*, Fogg Art Museum, Harvard University Art Museums, Cambridge, Massachusetts

1992   *On the Edge: Forty Years of Maine Painting*, Maine Coast Artists, Rockport

SELECTED COLLECTIONS

- University of Missouri
- University of Southern Maine, Gorham
- Fogg Art Museum
- Colby College Museum of Art, Waterville, Maine
- Albertina Museum, Vienna, Austria

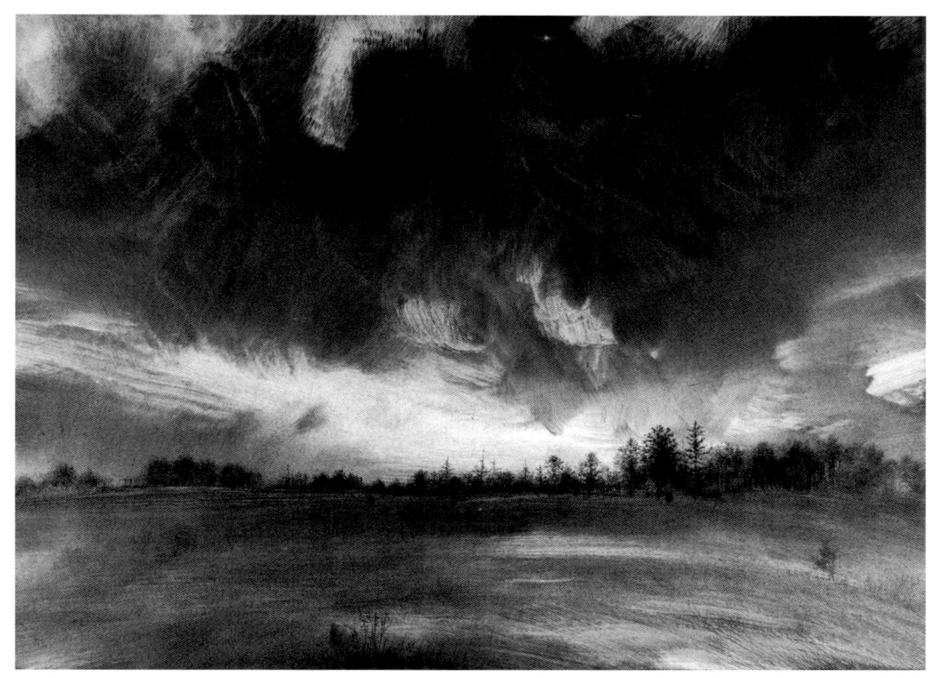

I would like my paintings to invite the viewer to proceed from the specific reality of the external, physical landscape into a space that is at once more intensely personal, mysterious, and perhaps mystical (spiritual).

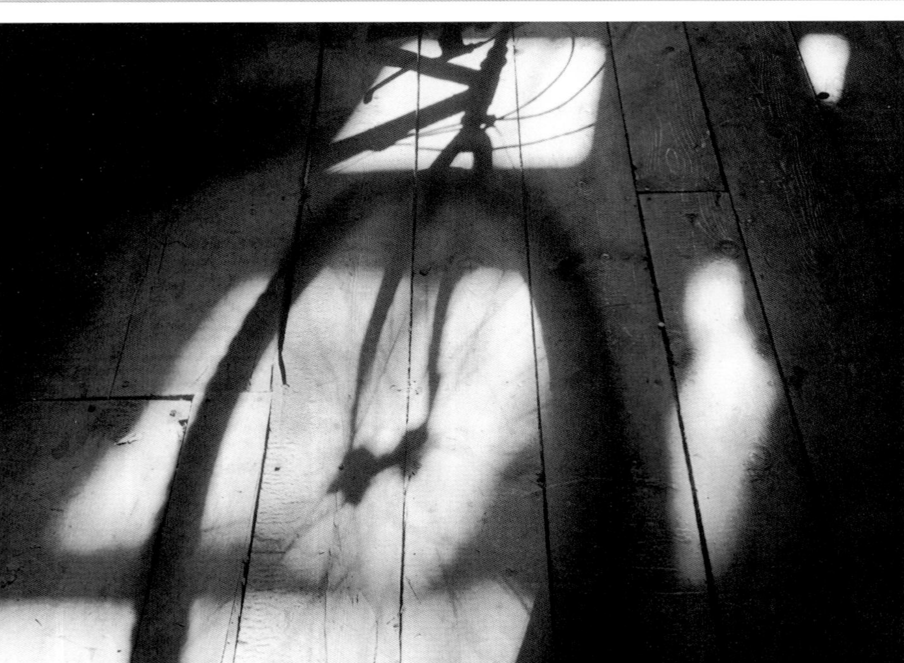

CYCLETTE #13
1998
gelatin silver print
18½ x 22½ inches

EDUCATION

1975   Apprenticeship in Photography, Manchester, New Hampshire
1973   Scranton School of Art, Pennsylvania
1970   Ringling School of Art, Sarasota, Florida

In my photography I try to capture light and other forms of radiant energy to produce an image that takes on a true power of its own that can be felt by the viewer.

BORN: 1945, Winthrop, MA

RESIDENCE: Portland, ME

SUMMER REV
1997
oil on plywood
24 x 20 inches

EDUCATION

1969 M.F.A., Painting, Yale University School of Art, New Haven, Connecticut

1967 B.F.A., Painting, Rhode Island School of Design, Providence

HONORS AND AWARDS

1995 Elizabeth Foundation Grant, New York

1994 Pollock-Krasner Foundation Grant Award, New York

SELECTED SOLO EXHIBITIONS

1996 *George Lloyd—Paintings*, Caldbeck Gallery, Rockland, Maine

1994 *George Lloyd—The Bay Area Years 1971-1982*, Kennedy Art Gallery, Holy Names College, Oakland, California

1993 Greenhut Gallery, Portland, Maine

SELECTED GROUP EXHIBITIONS

1999 *Drawing without Models*, Wiegand Gallery, Notre Dame College, Belmont, California

1996 *The Invented Figure*, Chuck Levitan Gallery, New York

1994 *The Breakfast Group, 20th Anniversary Show*, Landes Gallery, Berkeley, California

1992 *167th Annual Exhibition*, National Academy of Design, New York

SELECTED COLLECTIONS

- Achenbach Foundation, Palace of the Legion of Honor, San Francisco
- de Saisset Museum, University of Santa Clara, California
- Oakland Museum, California
- Ogunquit Museum of American Art, Maine
- Portland Museum of Art, Maine

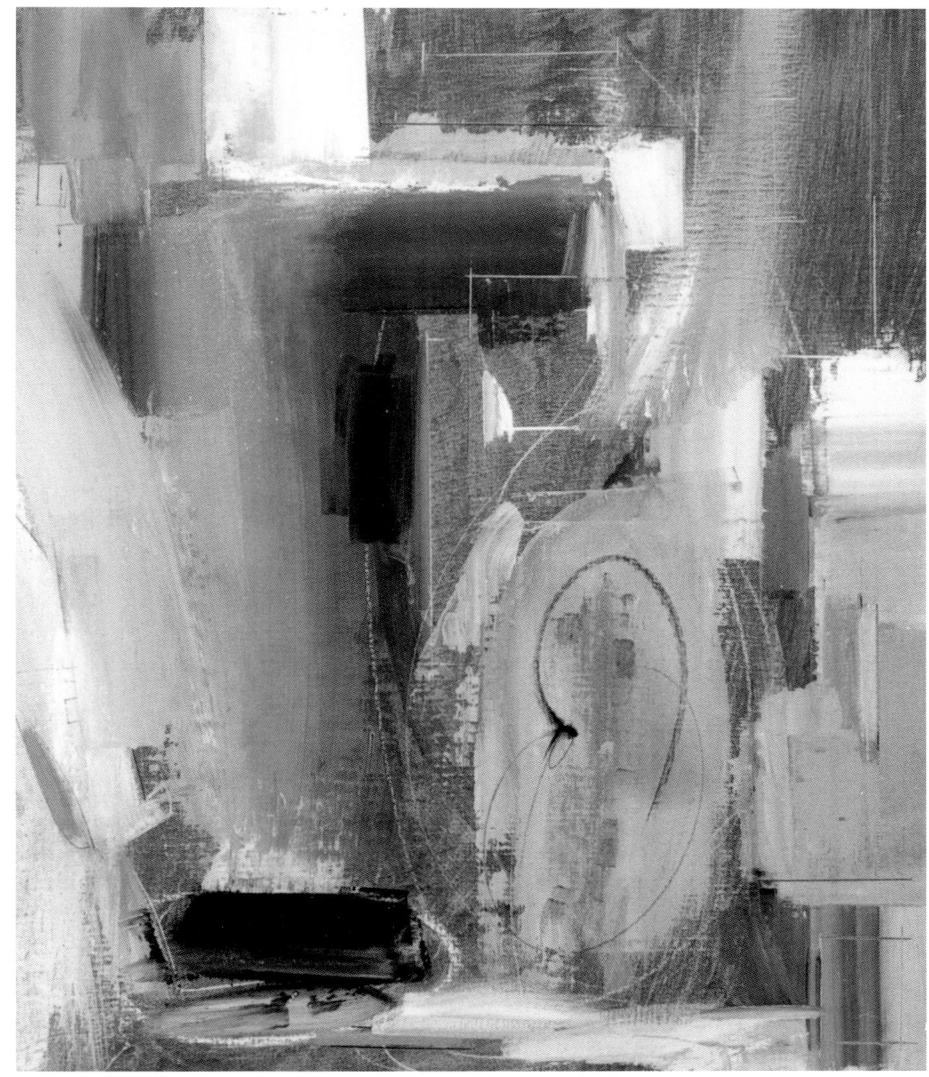

For the past several years I have oftentimes been working in the Venetian manner on dark grounds, a practice that has given, perhaps, an increasingly baroque character to my work. Figures and other organic elements have also made their way into an otherwise rectilinear structural framework. For two years now I have been working in oil again, after a hiatus of nearly 20 years. The differences from acrylic paint, although subtle, are proving to be significant, and I am experiencing a renewed vigor as well as a greater feeling of sensual enjoyment in the painting process.

GARRY MITCHELL

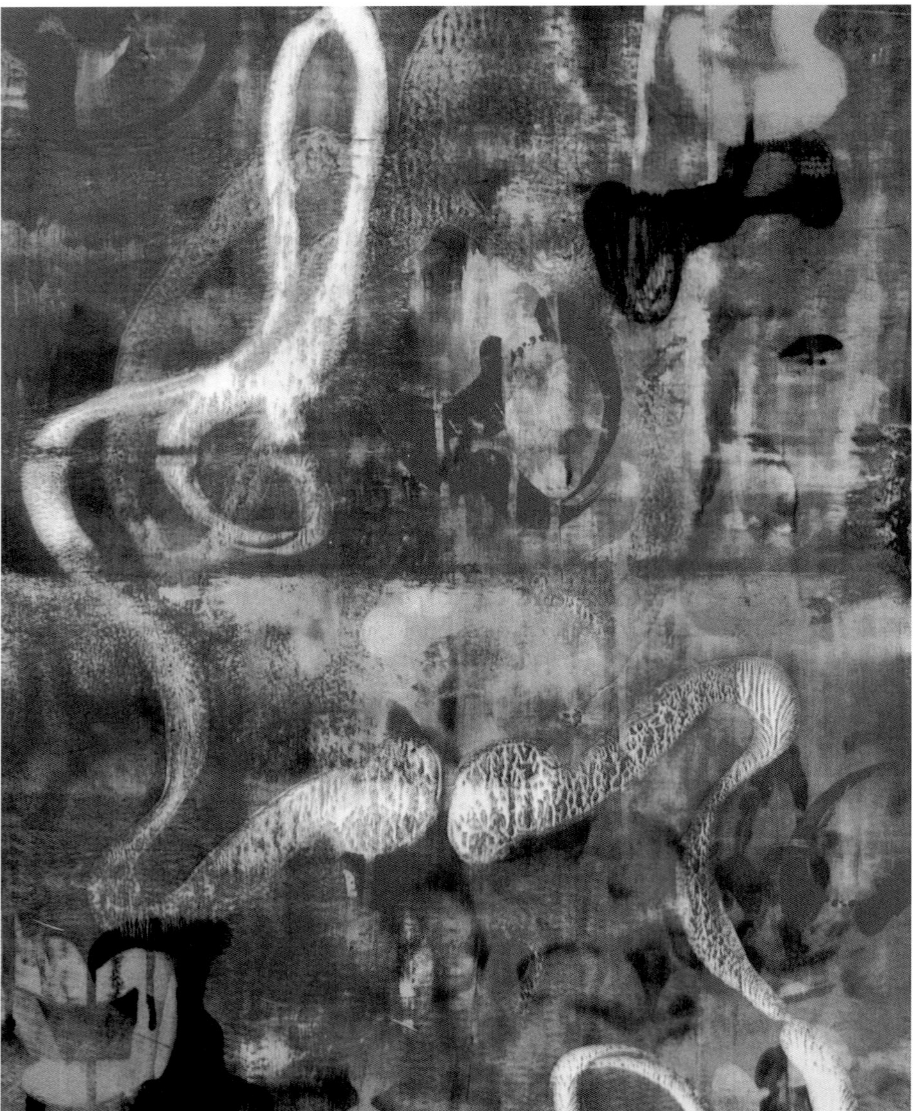

UNTITLED 2
1998
alkyd and wax on canvas
20 x 16 inches

EDUCATION

1982	M.F.A., Pratt Institute, Brooklyn, New York
1978	B.F.A., University of Hawaii, Honolulu

HONORS AND AWARDS

1997	Artists Residency, Yaddo, Saratoga Springs, New York
1997	Juror's Award, *New American Talent*, Texas Fine Art Association, Austin
1995	Individual Artists Grant, Maryland State Arts Council
1995	Esteban Vincente Endowed Fellowship, Yaddo

SELECTED SOLO EXHIBITIONS

1998	*3-D Design*, New York
1998	Maine Coast Artists, Rockport
1997	Takara Gallery, Houston, Texas
1992	Universal Fine Objects Gallery, Provincetown, Massachusetts

SELECTED GROUP EXHIBITIONS

1998	*Artists on Campus*, Maine Art Gallery, Wiscasset
1997	*New American Talent*, Texas Fine Art Association
1997	*Baltimore Collects*, Villa Julie College, Maryland
1997	*Faculty Exhibit*, Colby College Museum of Art, Waterville, Maine
1996	*Four Artists*, Harbor Gallery, University of Massachusetts, Boston

These images are found on the way to making something else, often not at all what I expected. They are, however, held together by a long chain of experiences that exist because of the struggle for resolution. It's a process of trial-and-error based on the faith that painting can be both evocative and straightforward, simultaneously conjuring up the world beyond its edges while seeming to tell nothing more than the story of its making. The hope is for work that exists between randomness and control, the intuitive and systematic, the hidden as well as the obvious.

BORN: 1927, Manchester, NH

RESIDENCE: Waldoboro, ME

ISLAND NEAR OWL'S HEAD
1997
watercolor on paper
14½ x 21 inches

EDUCATION
- Studied at University of New Hampshire, Durham and New England School of Art, Boston

HONORS AND AWARDS
- Dolphin Fellow, American Watercolor Society, New York
- National Academy of Design, New York
- National Watercolor Society, California
- Allied Artists of America, New York
- Audubon Artists, New York

SELECTED SOLO EXHIBITIONS
- Copley Society, Boston
- Doll and Richards, Boston
- Guild of Boston Artists
- Philadelphia Art Alliance, Pennsylvania
- Walt Kuhn Gallery, Cape Neddick, Maine

SELECTED GROUP EXHIBITIONS
- American Embassy, Ottawa, Canada
- Museum of Fine Arts, Boston
- Bowdoin College Museum of Art, Brunswick, Maine
- The Butler Institute of American Art, Youngstown, Ohio
- Metropolitan Museum of Art, New York

SELECTED COLLECTIONS
- First National Bank, Boston
- Farnsworth Art Museum, Rockland, Maine
- The Butler Institute of American Art
- Aetna Life Insurance, Hartford, Connecticut

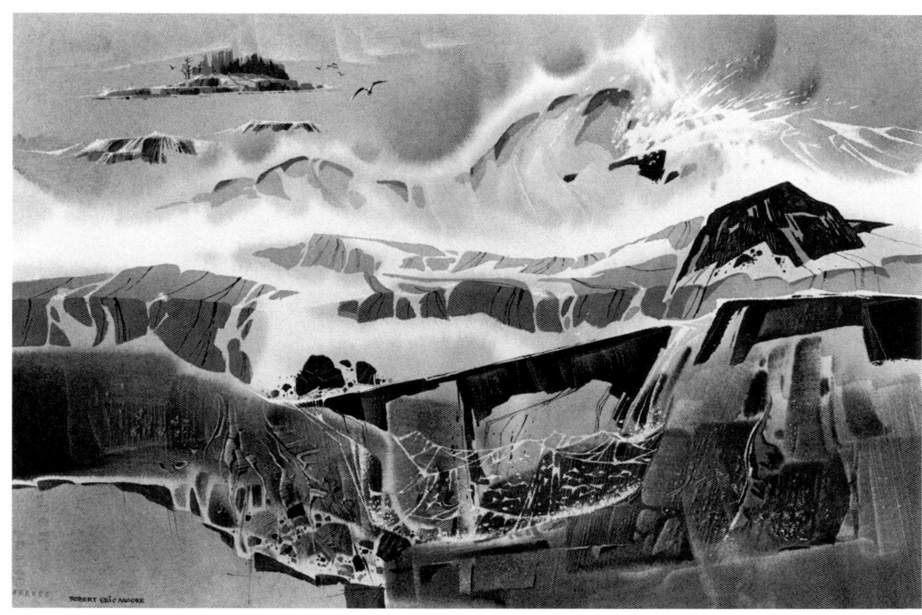

Painting has always been an extremely personal and private experience for me. Having grown up in New England I was very close to nature as a young boy and have kept that connection. The environment holds endless wonders to observe and be a part of. In nature I always see the interplay of strong abstract forms with subtle details. Looking at any scene there is a dynamic tension of light, air, motion, color, and texture; it is an experience of all the senses being awakened at once. The challenge I find in painting is to capture some of the dynamism, the movement, the subtlety, the constant moments of change.

BARBARA PETTER PUTNAM

RESIDENCE: Southborough, MA (Summer Residence: Deer Isle, ME)   BORN: 1954, Worcester, MA

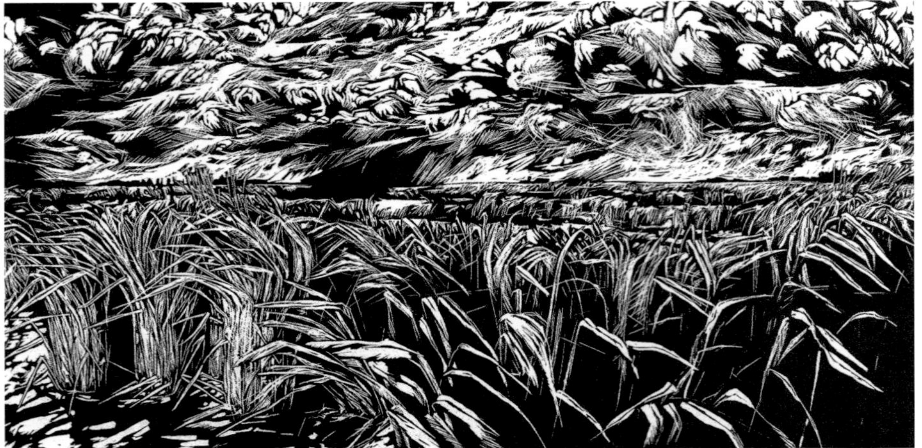

PRAIRIE STORM, MANITOBA
1997
woodcut on paper
24 x 48 inches

I see the making of art as research. Formally, I am interested in light and movement, which, along with the directness and simplicity of black-and-white woodcut, are my tools to explore the complex botanical habitat of wetlands. Woodcut for me is drawing, a way to respond to what I see with a candor that comes from the spontaneity of the materials.

EDUCATION

1985   A.L.M., Fine Arts, Harvard University, Cambridge, Massachusetts
1977   B.S., Art Education, University of New Hampshire, Durham

HONORS AND AWARDS

1997   Harvard Club Book Prize for teaching excellence, faculty vote, William Barber Faculty Chair, St. Marks School, Southborough, Massachusetts

SELECTED SOLO EXHIBITIONS

1997   *Magnificent*, Fletcher/Priest Gallery, Worcester, Massachusetts

SELECTED GROUP EXHIBITIONS

1998   *Minnesota National Print Biennial*, Katherine E. Nash Gallery, Minneapolis
1997   *Florida Printmakers Society 9th National Exhibition*, Jacksonville
1996   *Indiana Invitational*, Ball State Museum of Art, Muncie
1996   *Contemporary Printmaking*, Worcester Art Museum, Massachusetts
1996   *18th International Independent Exhibition of Prints*, Kanagawa, Japan

SELECTED COLLECTIONS

- Worcester Art Museum
- The Art Institute of Chicago
- Minneapolis Institute of Arts
- Fogg Art Museum, Harvard University Art Museums
- Yale University Art Gallery, New Haven, Connecticut

BORN: 1946, Stamford, CT

RESIDENCE: Cambridge, MA

NEAR COLFAX, WASHINGTON (8)
1996
dye coupler print
40 x 48 inches

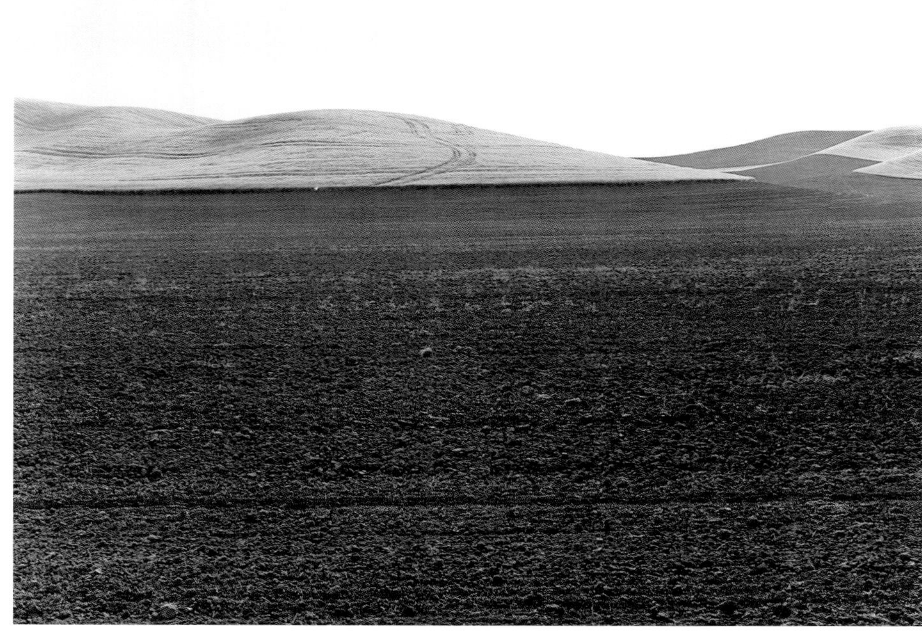

EDUCATION

1973   M.F.A., Photography, Rhode Island School of Design, Providence

1971   B.F.A., Photography, minor in Painting, Rhode Island School of Design

HONORS AND AWARDS

1989-98 Ilford Photo Corporation, Materials Grant

1985-98 Polaroid Corporation, Materials Grant

1996   Northeastern University, Boston, Faculty Development Fund

SELECTED SOLO EXHIBITIONS

1996   *The American Landscape*, Harvard Pilgrim Health Plan, Boston

1995   *A Special Place, Landscape Photographs of Martha's Vineyard*, The Vineyard Museum, Edgartown, Massachusetts

1995   *Recent Work*, Buckingham Brown and Nichols School, Cambridge, Massachusetts

1993   Center for Creative Imaging, Camden, Maine

SELECTED GROUP EXHIBITIONS

1998   *The Ernst Haas Memorial Collection*, Portland Museum of Art, Maine

1997   *11 Artists*, Photographic Resource Center, Boston

1997   *Digital Prints: The New Fine Art*, Concord Art Association, Massachusetts

1996   *The AIDS Portraits*, Pulse Art Gallery, New York

1996   *Silvertraces*, State Transportation Building Gallery, Boston

SELECTED COLLECTIONS

- Addison Gallery of American Art, Andover, Massachusetts
- Bibliotheque Nationale, Paris
- Center for Creative Photography, Tucson, Arizona
- Museum of Fine Arts, Boston
- Portland Museum of Art

Since being a student I have worked within the discipline of black-and-white photography. Through many projects and portfolios I have maintained a prevailing interest in how things look when photographed. While individual sets and series have had more specific intent, overall my work is characterized by a concern for photographic quality, a formalistic interest stemming from studies in design; a sense of wonder in the naturally occurring oddities, incongruities, and inconsequential things in this world; a preoccupation with light; and a love of the medium of photography.

While I in no way feel finished at the age of 51, I do feel I've at least accomplished one of my objectives since I started in the early '70s. That was to produce a body of work of high quality. Since then I have made countless pictures and many sets and series. Much of my teaching over all these years has been to bring students into photography on the premise that they would learn about seeing. As I reflect upon 25 years of my compulsion to make photographs I realize that my work too is very much about seeing. By using photography to capture parts of the world that interest me I can relate to my surroundings in truly substantial ways and bring back home those places, events and qualities that I cannot bear to be without and then share them with others.

LORNA J. RITZ

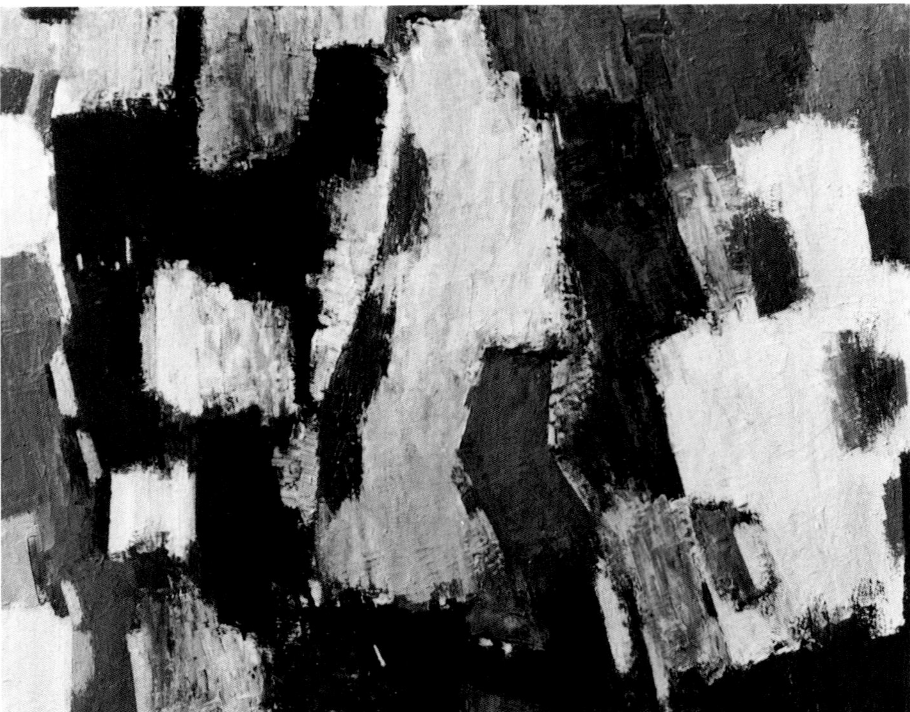

LIGHT AND SHADOW ON SNOW
1998
oil on linen
48 x 60 inches

Each of my paintings represents a crystallized chunk of formal experience, yet they are very personal at the same time. My paintings are earthy, rock-like, and weighty, and yet they have in them the rhythm of the sea. I am a nature painter; the nature "out there," coupled with my own internal landscape. My "inner" finds the equivalent "out there."

I search for the structure and form through the relationship of colors. I am interested in the vibration that occurs when the edge of one color touches that of another. They define each other by not being the same, but of a particular quality that allows them to pull apart spatially, creating the illusion of depth on the flat surface of linen. This process of painting evolves through improvisation, a constant removal and replacement of colors that manifest an inner sense of illumination.

It has taken me all this time to realize that I paint the seasons as they are occurring. My eye translates directly to my hands. I also paint captured memories of travels into unfamiliar cultures. Temperature ranges and feelings are relived through my process of painting, trying to locate as much essence as possible.

EDUCATION

1971   M.F.A., Painting and Sculpture, Cranbrook Academy of Art, Bloomfield Hills, Michigan

1969   B.F.A., Painting, minor in Sculpture, Pratt Institute, Brooklyn, New York

1968   Skowhegan School of Painting and Sculpture, Maine

HONORS AND AWARDS

1998   Residency to Fundacion Valparaiso, Almeria, Spain

1997   Pollock-Krasner Foundation Grant Award, New York

SELECTED SOLO EXHIBITIONS

1998   University Gallery, Fine Arts Center, University of Massachusetts, Amherst

1995   Gallery B.A.I., New York

1995   Bowery Gallery, New York

1994   Hillyer Gallery, Smith College, Northampton, Massachusetts

SELECTED GROUP EXHIBITIONS

1998   Marlen Gallery, New York

1997   La Mama La Galleria, New York

1996   Bristol Art Museum, Rhode Island

1995   Creiger-Dane Gallery, Boston

1993   *Art in Embassies Program*, Washington, DC; Banjoul, the Gambia; Valette, Malta; Praia, Cape Verde

SELECTED COLLECTIONS

- Bank of Boston & International Bank of New England
- Mount Holyoke College Art Museum, South Hadley, Massachusetts
- High Voltage Engineering, Shrafts Center, Boston
- Biogen Corporation, Cambridge, Massachusetts
- Anderson Contemporary Art, Taos, New Mexico

BORN: 1951, Biddeford, ME

RESIDENCE: Gainesville, FL (Summer Residence: Portland, ME)

STACK
1998
antique chaise lounge and slate
48 x 72 x 27 inches

EDUCATION

1986	M.F.A., Nova Scotia College of Art and Design, Halifax
1979	Skowhegan School of Painting and Sculpture, Maine
1979	B.F.A., Portland School of Art (now Maine College of Art)
1975	B.A., Sociology, University of Maine, Orono

HONORS AND AWARDS

1998	Pollack-Krasner Foundation Grant Award, New York
1998	Fine Arts and Humanities Scholarship Enhancement Award, University of Florida, Gainesville
1996	Teaching Award, University of Florida
1996	Research Development Award, University of Florida
1995	New Faculty Research Grant, University of Florida

SELECTED SOLO EXHIBITIONS

1998	*STACKS*, Adair Margo Gallery, El Paso, Texas
1997	*STACKS*, ARC Gallery, Chicago
1996	*Celeste Roberge: Sculpture*, Nations Bank Plaza, Tampa, Florida
1995	*Geographies Geologies Anatomies*, Maine Coast Artists, Rockport
1993	*The Mind is a Muscle*, Farnsworth Art Museum, Rockland, Maine

SELECTED GROUP EXHIBITIONS

1998	*Drawn from Nature*, Dalton Gallery, Agnes Scott College, Decatur, Georgia
1996	*Skowhegan at 50: The Maine Legacy*, Maine Coast Artists, Rockport and the Baxter Gallery, Maine College of Art
1995	*Contemporary Sculpture at Chesterwood*, Stockbridge, Massachusetts
1995	*Sculpture on the Grounds*, Florida Gulf Coast Art Center, Belleair
1994	*Migrant Within*, University of Maine Museum of Art, Orono

SELECTED COLLECTIONS

- Runnymede Sculpture Farm, Woodside, California
- Gardner Group, Santa Barbara, California
- Portland Museum of Art, Maine
- Farnsworth Art Museum
- Samuel P. Harn Museum of Art, University of Florida

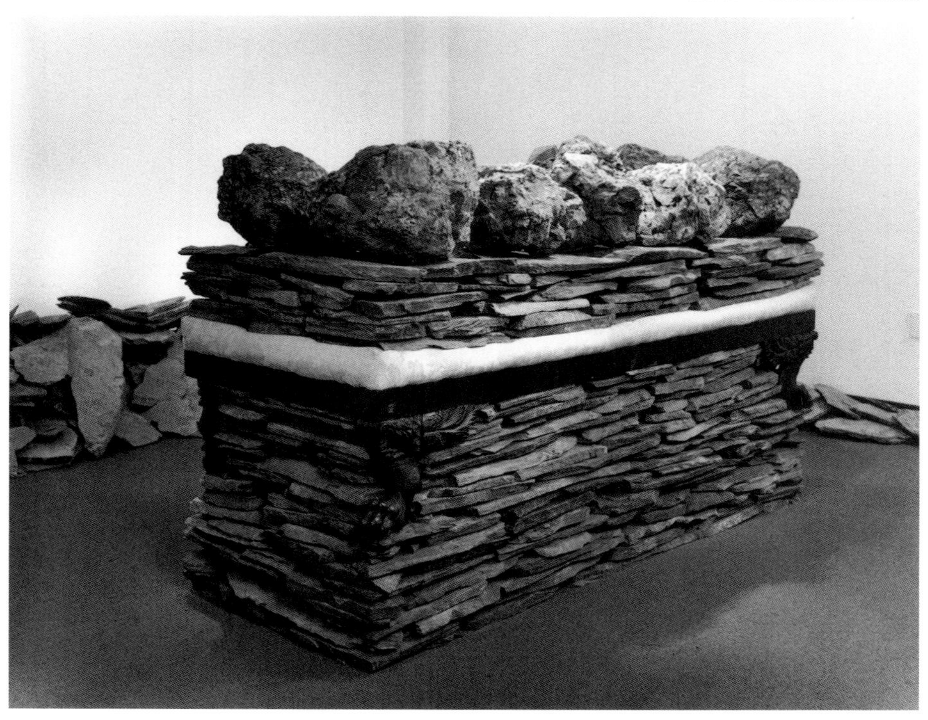

The subject of this work is the embeddedness of artifacts. Although we like to imagine that artifacts born of human imagination exist free from time and decay, the material conditions of the world inevitably recoup them. These sculptures, built upon the furniture and architecture of yesterday, create a self-conscious archaeology that refers to burial, stratification, and fossilization. The labor evident in stacking the tons of stone makes the process of cultural sedimentation physically present to the viewer and establishes a link between human and geological time.

The STACKS series consists of antique daybeds, chaise lounges, and chairs that are separately embedded in several tons of dry-stacked stone. The form of each STACK is determined by the form of the artifact and an absent human body.

The origin of this series lies in my fascination with the archaic architecture of Turkey, Egypt, and Mexico, with stone walls of New England and the prehistoric structures of Northern Europe. At the many archaic sites I have visited, the processes of nature and culture have become blurred as the architecture has weathered and become embedded in natural history. STACKS also relates to the art historical tradition of the reclining figure, such as Canova's Neoclassical sculpture *Pauline Borghese as Venus Victorious*, which along with the architectural and geological associations compresses the archaic, the neoclassical, and the late modern into the experience of the sculpture.

LIV KRISTIN ROBINSON

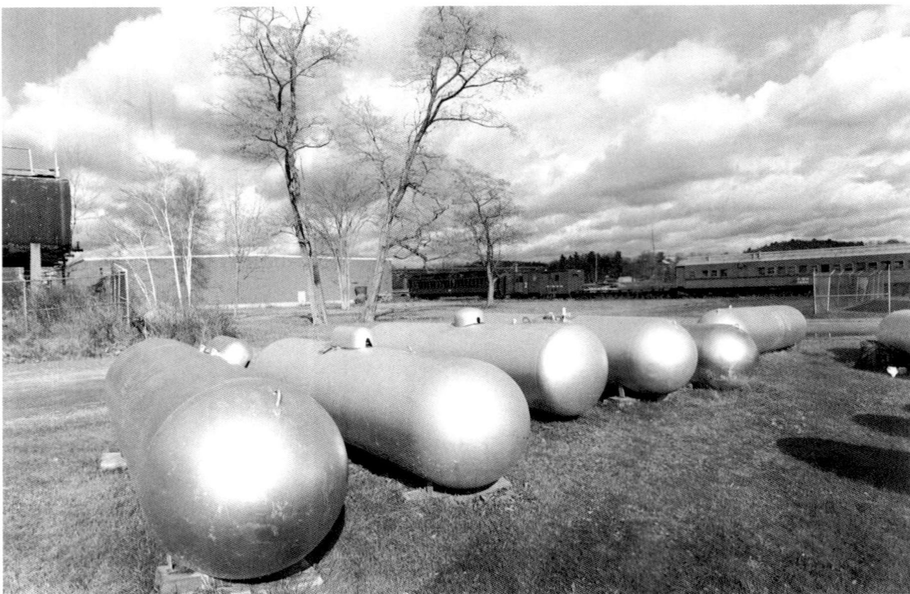

BELFAST WATERFRONT (#5)
1996
oil pigment on toned gelatin silver print
22 x 24 inches

In August of 1988 I had the good fortune to meet Berenice Abbott when she exhibited her photographs of New York at what was then Gallery 68 in Belfast. I told her I grew up in New York, had just moved to Belfast in 1986, and was photographing its 19th-century residential architecture. In a few terse words she dismissed my current efforts. "If I were you," she admonished, "I would concentrate on the industrial buildings and the waterfront. It's what's really important, and it's changing, you know!"

I thought a lot then about the link between Belfast's evolving cultural life and its working industrial waterfront. So many artists had moved to the Belfast area in the 1970s and '80s precisely because of depressed real estate prices. I began to pursue new directions in my own work. On my walks along the edges of town I was now drawn to the formal elements and relationships in the structures I saw—shapes and lines, color and texture. Looking closely at this seemingly discarded section of town is something I have enjoyed doing over the last ten years.

EDUCATION

1986   The Maine Photographic Workshops, Rockport (also 1990)

1985   International Center of Photography, New York

1975   M.A., Art History, Institute of Fine Arts, New York University, New York

1971   B.A., Art History, Hunter College, New York

HONORS AND AWARDS

1995   Best in Show, *Biennial Photo Exhibit*, University of Maine Museum of Art, Orono

SELECTED SOLO EXHIBITIONS

1998   *Belfast: On the Waterfront*, Abbott Room, Belfast, Maine

1996   *Belfast...On the Edge*, Maine Coast Artists, Rockport

1993   Art Center, Palos Verdes, California

SELECTED GROUP EXHIBITIONS

1997-98   *Aperture: Contemporary Maine Photography on the Edge of Process*, Arts in the Capital Series, Augusta, Maine

1995   Frick Gallery, Belfast, Maine

1995   *Biennial Photo Exhibit*, University of Maine Museum of Art, Orono

1995   *War*, Union of Maine Visual Artists, Ellsworth and Bangor Public Libraries

1992   The Maine Art Gallery, Wiscasset Art Gallery, Unity College, Maine

SELECTED COLLECTIONS

- Colby College Museum of Art, Waterville, Maine
- Farnsworth Art Museum, Rockland, Maine

TWELVE CORNERS
1996
egg tempera on panels
30 x 90 inches

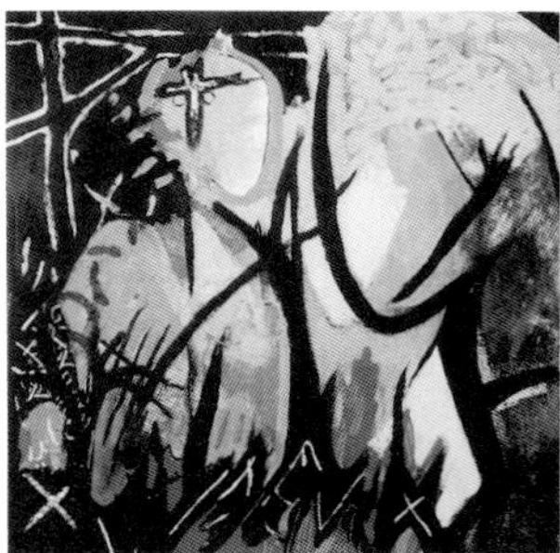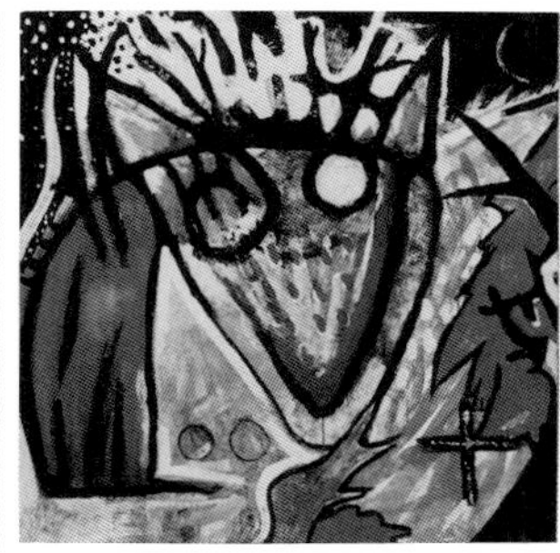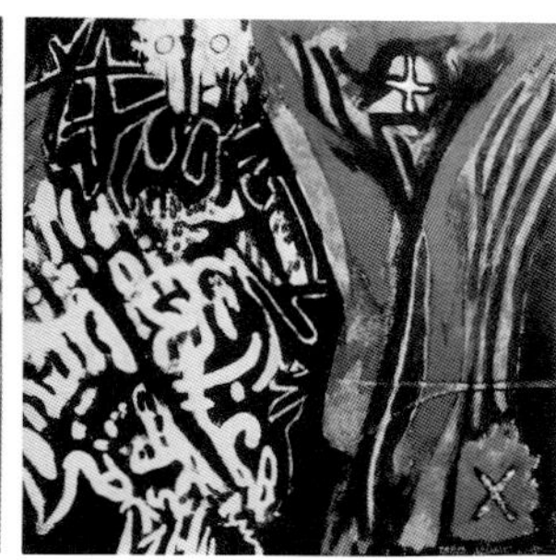

EDUCATION

1960-62 Art Students League, New York
1960-62 Pratt Graphics Center, New York
1961　Skowhegan School of Painting and
　　　Sculpture, Maine (also 1959)
1960　California School of Fine Arts, San Francisco
1958-59 Reed College, Portland, Oregon

SELECTED SOLO EXHIBITIONS

1997　*Recent Work*, Caldbeck Gallery, Rockland,
　　　Maine
1996　*12 Corners*, June Fitzpatrick Gallery,
　　　Portland, Maine
1994　*Hibernation*, Caldbeck Gallery

SELECTED GROUP EXHIBITIONS

1997　*The Eccentric Image*, Icon Contemporary
　　　Art, Brunswick, Maine
1996　*Skowhegan at 50: The Maine Legacy*,
　　　Maine Coast Artists, Rockport
　　　and the Baxter Gallery, Maine College of
　　　Art, Portland
1995　*A Family of Artists: 3 Generations*, Anne
　　　Reid Art Gallery, Princeton, New Jersey
1992　*On the Edge: Forty Years of Maine Painting*,
　　　Maine Coast Artists
1993　*Multiple Dialogues*, The Painted Bride Art
　　　Center, Philadelphia

SELECTED COLLECTIONS

* Colby College Museum of Art,
  Waterville, Maine
* Bowdoin College Museum of Art,
  Brunswick, Maine
* Farnsworth Art Museum, Rockland, Maine
* Portland Museum of Art, Maine
* Hirshhorn Museum and Sculpture Garden,
  Washington, DC

For the last several years I've been working in a manner where I have started abstract and allowed images to emerge from the paint. I have found these images to have a degree of honesty and depth which seemed greater than that which I arrived at by more intentional methods.

Most of my work is arrived at in this manner, with the exception of *Twelve Corners*, which was painted in direct response to a tragic car crash.

MICHAEL SHAUGHNESSY

RESIDENCE: Windham, ME

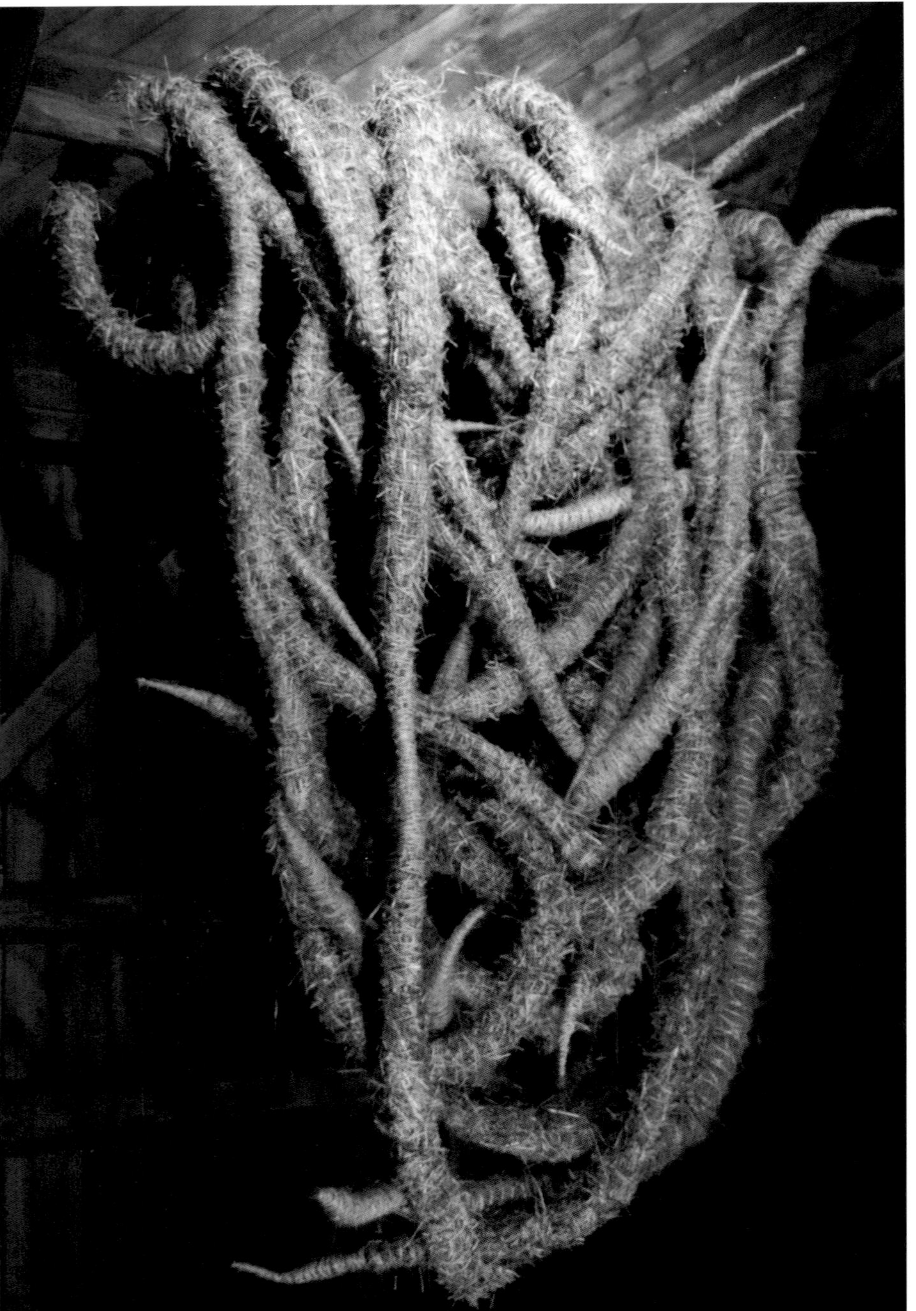

POMONI'S LOOP AND FALL, SECOND VARIATION
1998
hay and twine
120 x 72 x 36 inches

EDUCATION
1984   M.F.A., Ohio University, Athens
1981   B.A., University of Missouri, Kansas City

HONORS AND AWARDS
1995   Individual Artist Grant, New England Foundation for the Arts
1995   Maine Arts Commission Fellowship

SELECTED SOLO EXHIBITIONS
1998   Kemper Museum of Art, Kansas City, Missouri
1997   Indiana State University, Terre Haute
1996   Rice University, Houston, Texas
1996   Wheaton College, Norton, Massachusetts
1996   Elgin Community College, Illinois
1994   *Branwen's Triad*, Delaware Center for Contemporary Art, Wilmington

SELECTED GROUP EXHIBITIONS
1997   *KC/3D*, Forum for Contemporary Art, St. Louis, Missouri
1995   *PERSPECTIVES: A Sense of Place*, Portland Museum of Art, Maine
1994   *Garden of Sculptural Delights*, Exit Art/First World, New York
1994   *Private Libraries: Watershed Colloquy*, University of Southern Maine Art Gallery, Gorham
1993   *Ideas of Nature*, UMF Art Gallery, University of Maine, Farmington

Differing from my larger woven works, *Pomoni's Loop and Fall, Second Variation* is from a body of work that is the result of binding many lines of hay, arranging, and rebinding again.

The lines are placed one over the other as if stored for future consideration and use. The process is immediate and intuitive, worked by acknowledgment as much as by design. It is a simple and direct combination of material, repetition, context, and my own intuition and sensibilities.

TONGUE
1997
oil on wood
36 x 36 inches

EDUCATION
1986 M.F.A., Painting, Pratt Institute, New York
1980 B.A., Studio Art, Painting,
      Wesleyan University, Middletown,
      Connecticut
1979 Temple University Abroad, Rome
1978 Tyler School of Art, Philadelphia

HONORS AND AWARDS
1996 Fellowship, Bemis Center for the
      Contemporary Arts, Omaha, Nebraska

SELECTED SOLO EXHIBITIONS
1997 Meridian Gallery, San Francisco

SELECTED GROUP EXHIBITIONS
1998 *Challenge Exhibit Anniversary*, Samuel
      Fleisher Art Memorial, Philadelphia
1997 *Flesh and Blood*, Hewlett Gallery, Carnegie
      Mellon University, Pittsburgh
1997 *Dix Artistes Americaines*, Galerie Laiterie,
      Strasbourg, France
1997 *Invitational*, Maine Coast Artists, Rockport
1996 *9 Artists, 9 Visions*, DeCordova Museum
      and Sculpture Park, Lincoln, Massachusetts

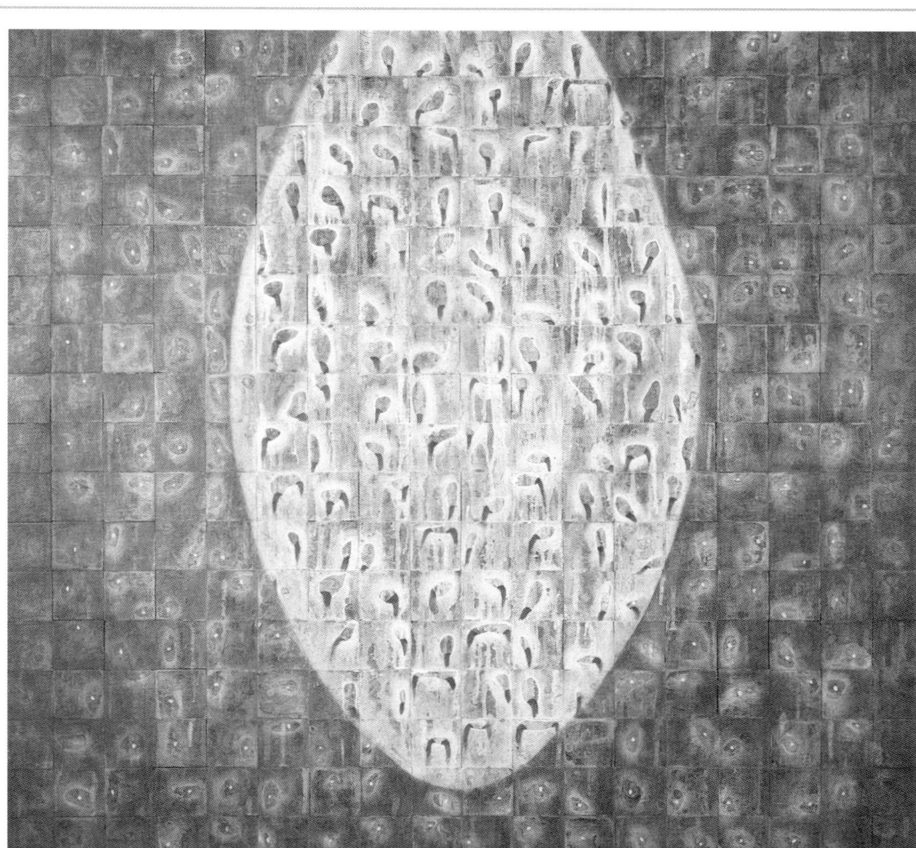

Underlying all of my creative work has been a solid interest in human experience—moral, psychological, personal, and political. My early large expressive figurative paintings have become, over time, a symbolically abstracted body—cells, neurons, veins, blood, milk, wounds, sutures, etc.... The body of my work remains centered on issues of life and death, family, women, and our environment. I draw from the sciences, literature, philosophy, current events, life experiences. I am interested in creating multiple readings, meanings, or interpretations of images and ideas. The earth amazes me in its regeneration, the human body in its recovery from disease. Our relationships continue to grow and prosper despite deep pains and sorrows; our beings continue to be tied to the natural world despite its wholesale destruction and abuse. These wonders motivate my work with its core themes of survival and regeneration.

Tongue and *Tongue 2* refer to a child's way of knowing the world, through the tongue, a place of sensory overload, erotic pleasure, and bodily satisfaction.

In the smaller canvas paintings, drawings, and prints, the concerns are the same. As in the larger works, I begin with a network of lines and shapes, which I then scrape off or paint over with succeeding networks of marks or forms. These are often removed as well, the process continuing on ad infinitum. Finally, what results is a mesh or web of interconnections of order and chance. Though both the destructive and constructive forces permeating our lives are visible in my work, my hope is to be ultimately life affirming.

ROBERT SOLOTAIRE

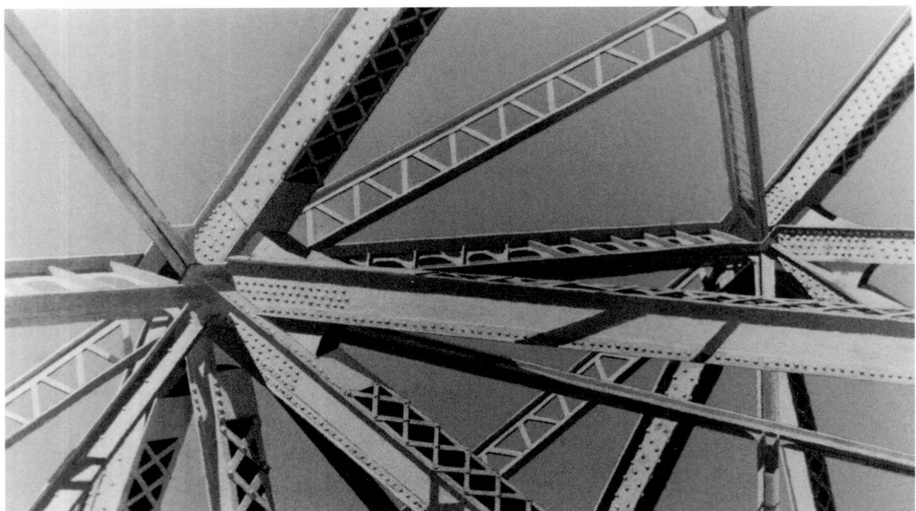

138TH ST. BRIDGE
1996
oil on paper
18 x 30 inches

EDUCATION
1952   Bard College, Annandale, New York
Art Students League, New York

SELECTED SOLO EXHIBITIONS
1996   Tom Veilleux Gallery, Farmington, Maine

SELECTED GROUP EXHIBITIONS
1998   *100th Anniversary of Greater New York*,
Gallery of Graphic Arts, New York
1997   *Realism in 20th-Century American Painting*,
Ogunquit Museum of American Art, Maine
1996   *New Jersey Center for the Visual Arts
International*, Summit
1992   *On the Edge: Forty Years of Maine Painting*,
Maine Coast Artists, Rockport

SELECTED COLLECTIONS
- Portland Museum of Art, Maine
- Farnsworth Art Museum, Rockland, Maine
- Casco Northern Bank (now KeyBank)
Portland, Maine
- Fleet Bank, Portland, Maine
- Mid-Maine Savings, Lewiston

BORN: 1958, Hartford, CT

RESIDENCE: South Portland, ME

THE STRUGGLE BETWEEN THE INTELLECT AND THE SPIRIT: JUST BEFORE DECIDING
1997
acrylic on panel
18 x 18 inches

EDUCATION

1986 Skowhegan School of Painting and Sculpture, Maine
1987 M.F.A., San Francisco Art Institute
1980 B.F.A., University of Southern Maine, Gorham

HONORS AND AWARDS

1996 Fellowship, Djerassi Foundation Resident Artists Program, Woodside, California

SELECTED GROUP EXHIBITIONS

1998 *Faculty Exhibition*, Institute of Contemporary Art, Maine College of Art, Portland
1998 *Talent in Abundance*, O'Farrell Gallery, Brunswick, Maine
1997 *Faculty Exhibition*, Colby College Museum of Art, Waterville, Maine
1997 *Picking up the Pieces*, Curated by Mary Harding, York, Maine
1997 *3 Painters, 2 Sculptors*, Between The Muse Gallery, Rockland, Maine

SELECTED COLLECTIONS

- Portland Museum of Art, Maine
- University of Southern Maine, Gorham
- City of Sakaide, Japan

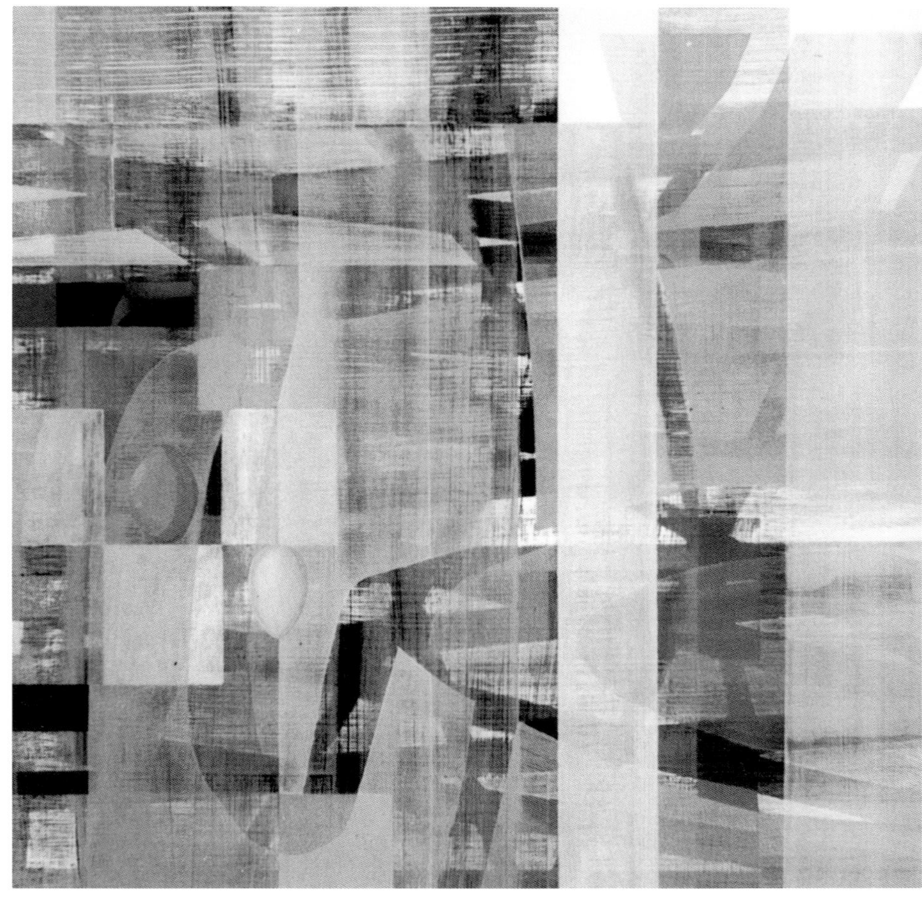

I have had a long-time preoccupation with the balance between abstraction and representation—between narrative and the painted surface. My solution to this preoccupation is to use a recognizable object or image fragment against an abstracted ground. Nothing is prearranged. I trust completely in the process and rely on the will of the paint to determine the outcome. I work up the structure of the painting by adding, subtracting, and weaving color, so that the illusion of space becomes more and more apparent. At a certain point in this process I look for areas where images and objects could go, place them in the painting, and enclose the space around them.

My primary subject is the character of space. I want viewers to physically slow down their looking and wind their way through a particular space and search to uncover something. The spaces I work with are derived from two geographies: the ocean with no sight of land, and the woods with no sight of a horizon line.

My secondary subject is a narrative which is derived from everyday life. By combining specific objects and image fragments into visual phases, my daily, ongoing, passing thoughts are constructed in a concrete visual form. My intent is to create an intimate experience which is suspended in time and contributes to our world as a contrast to the noise.

● ALICE SPENCER

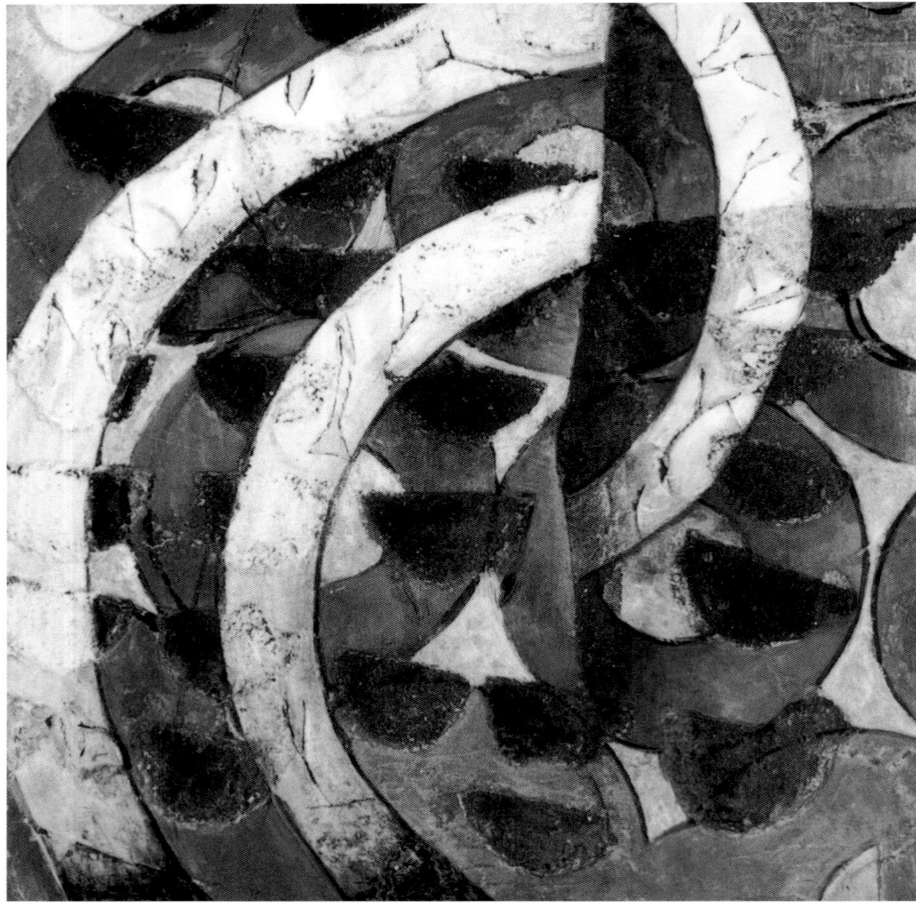

My current work takes as its point of departure the layered history suggested in shards of ancient pottery.

FRAGMENT WITH GREEN STRIPE
1998
plaster and acrylic on board
12 x 12 x 2½ inches

EDUCATION
1966   B.A., Sarah Lawrence College, Bronxville, New York
1966   San Francisco Art Institute

SELECTED SOLO EXHIBITIONS
1998   Watson Gallery, Wheaton College, Norton, Massachusetts
1997   June Fitzpatrick Gallery, Portland, Maine
1997   Judith Leighton Gallery, Blue Hill, Maine
1996   Between The Muse Gallery, Rockland, Maine
1995   Sunnen Gallery, New York

SELECTED GROUP EXHIBITIONS
1997   *Birds in Image and Imagination*, Wendell Gilley Museum, Southwest Harbor, Maine
1997   *Images in Multiple: Six Maine Women Printmakers*, State House Gallery, Augusta, Maine
1997   *Percent for Art: Maine's Public Art Legacy*, Blaine House, Augusta
1996   *Torn Asunder: Collage in Twentieth-Century Art*, Portland Museum of Art, Maine
1995   *PERSPECTIVES: A Sense of Place*, Portland Museum of Art

SELECTED COLLECTIONS
- Portland Museum of Art
- Colby College Museum of Art, Waterville, Maine
- Boston Athenaeum
- United Technologies, Hartford, Connecticut
- Ogunquit Museum of American Art, Maine

BEN'S BIKE
1997
oil on canvas
12 x 12 inches

EDUCATION

1958 B.F.A., Massachusetts College of Art, Boston

SELECTED GROUP EXHIBITIONS

1998 Gleason Fine Art, Boothbay Harbor, Maine
1997 *Concord Art Association Juried Show,* Massachusetts
1996 *Annual Juried Exhibition,* Maine Coast Artists, Rockport
1995 J.S. Ames Fine Art, Belfast, Maine
1995 The Copley Society of Boston

SELECTED COLLECTIONS

- Marriner Lumber, Brunswick, Maine
- MBNA, Camden, Maine and Wilmington, Delaware
- Douglas Richmond Architects, Brunswick, Maine
- Moss Inc., Belfast, Maine

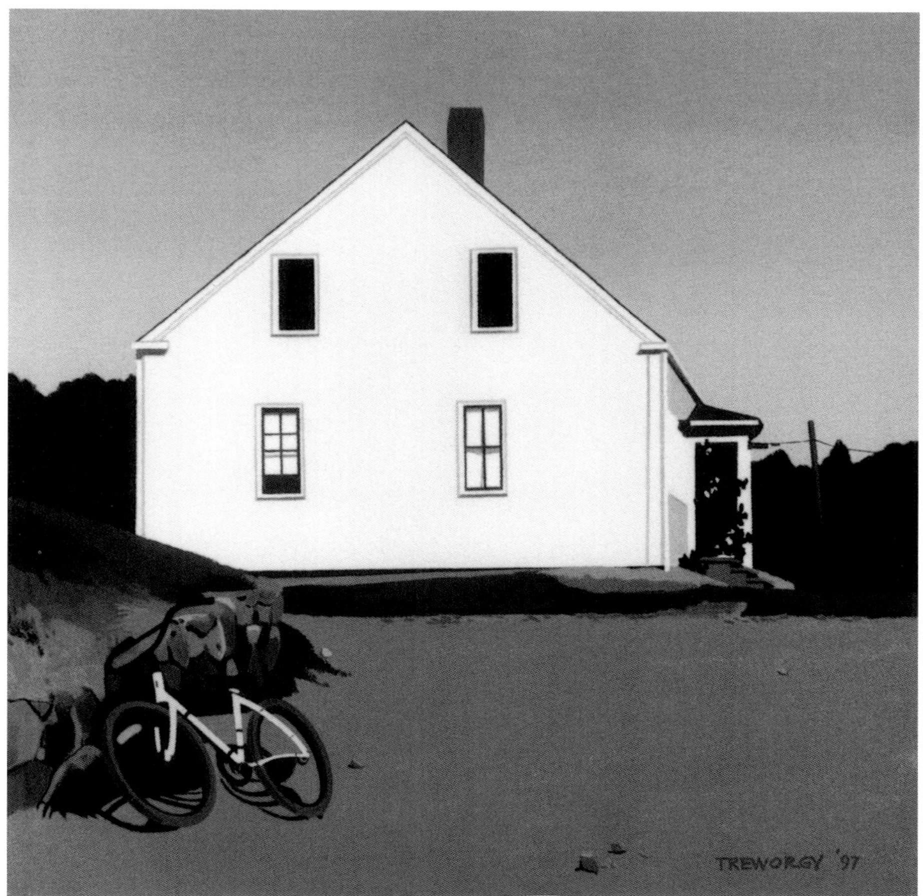

I work to capture the moment in my landscapes of buildings. These moments generally happen early in the morning or late in the afternoon, when the sun is low and causes dramatic shadows to fall across the landscapes, creating memorable patterns and relationships, and wide ranges of warm and cool colors and light and dark values. Even during the dark moments in the resolution of these issues on the canvas, I know that the original personal vision will carry me along to a satisfying conclusion.

FRANK VALLIERE

START ME UP
1997
oil pastel on paper
14 x 17 inches

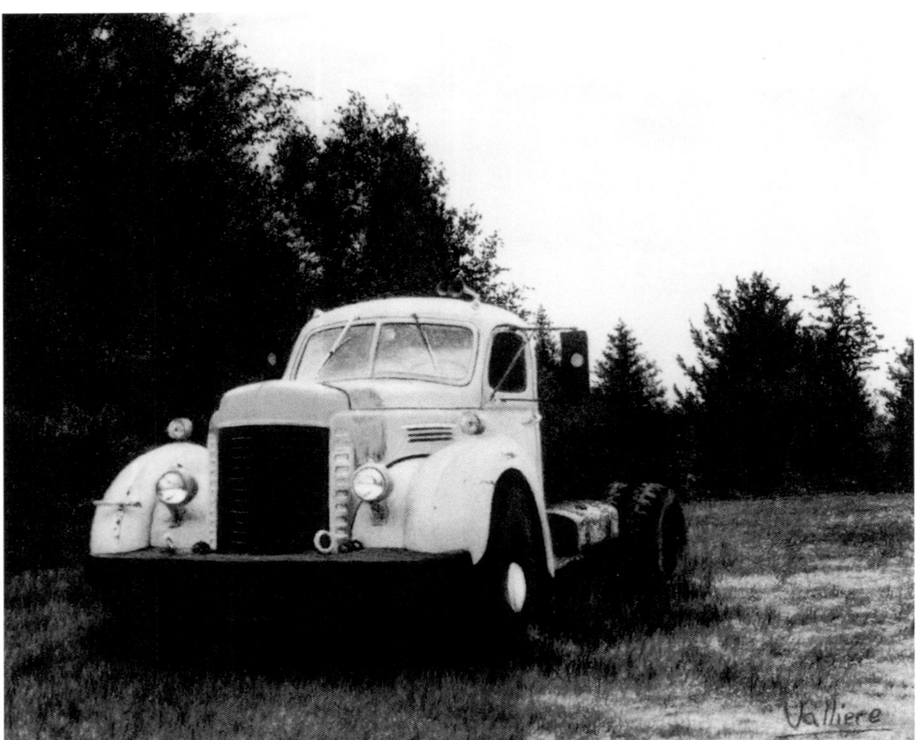

EDUCATION

1982   B.F.A., School of the Museum of Fine Arts, Boston, and Tufts University, Medford, Massachusetts

SELECTED GROUP EXHIBITIONS

1997   School of the Museum of Fine Arts Gallery, Boston

1996   Area Galley, University of Southern Maine, Portland

The bulk of my private study deals with a lifelong interest in the rural landscape. I am taken in by the different atmospheres, the random patterns and colors. Old buildings, vehicles, and other objects of the human existence left to the environment seem to be telling their stories: where they have been, what they have done, and what they are doing now, as they settle in for the long haul, taking on more and more the character of their surroundings—the harsh beautiful truth.

UNTITLED (THE EMPTY CUP RUNNETH OVER)
1998
oil on board
48 x 36 inches

EDUCATION

1985   M.F.A., San Francisco Art Institute
1983   B.A., Bowdoin College, Brunswick, Maine

HONORS AND AWARDS

1994   Fellowship, Djerassi Foundation Resident
       Artists Program, Woodside, California
1993   Maine Arts Commission Fellowship

SELECTED SOLO EXHIBITIONS

2000   Frye Art Museum, Seattle
1997   O.K. Harris Works of Art, New York
       (also 1995 and 1993)
1996   Horwitch-Newman Gallery, Phoenix,
       Arizona
1993   Bowdoin College Museum of Art

SELECTED GROUP EXHIBITIONS

1998   *Realism 98,* van de Griff Gallery, Santa Fe,
       New Mexico
1996   *Highlights from the Permanent Collection,*
       Knoxville Museum of Art, Tennessee
1996   *Real/Unreal,* Horwitch-Newman Gallery
1996   *9 Visions, 9 Artists,* DeCordova Museum
       and Sculpture Park, Lincoln, Massachusetts
1996   *Certain Uncertainties: Chaos and the
       Human Experience,* Bowdoin College
       Museum of Art

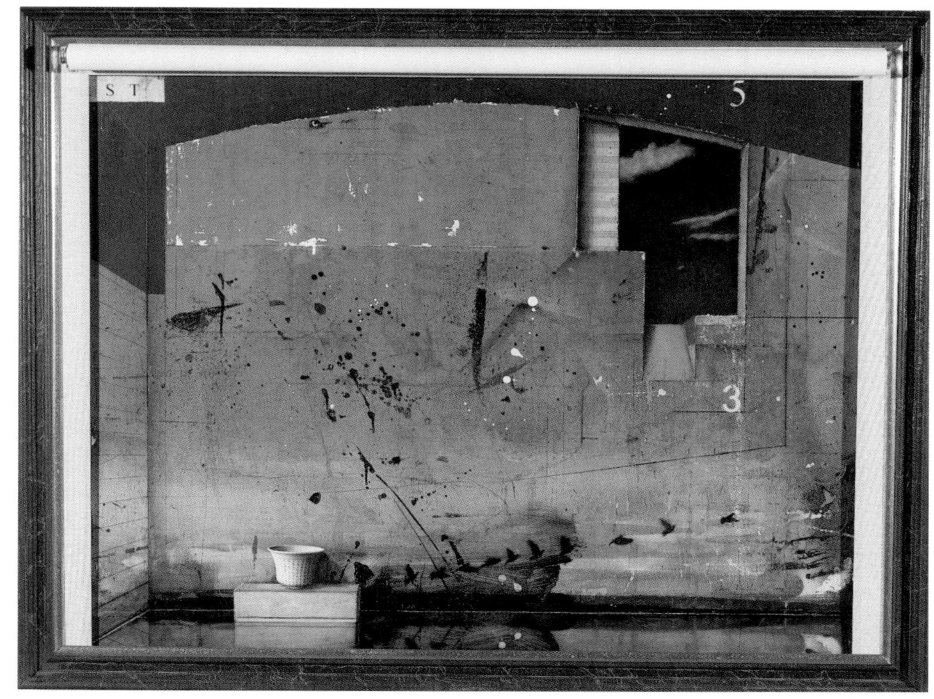

Trust your own experience, it is exactly right. There is nothing extra that you need to know.

DAVID WADE

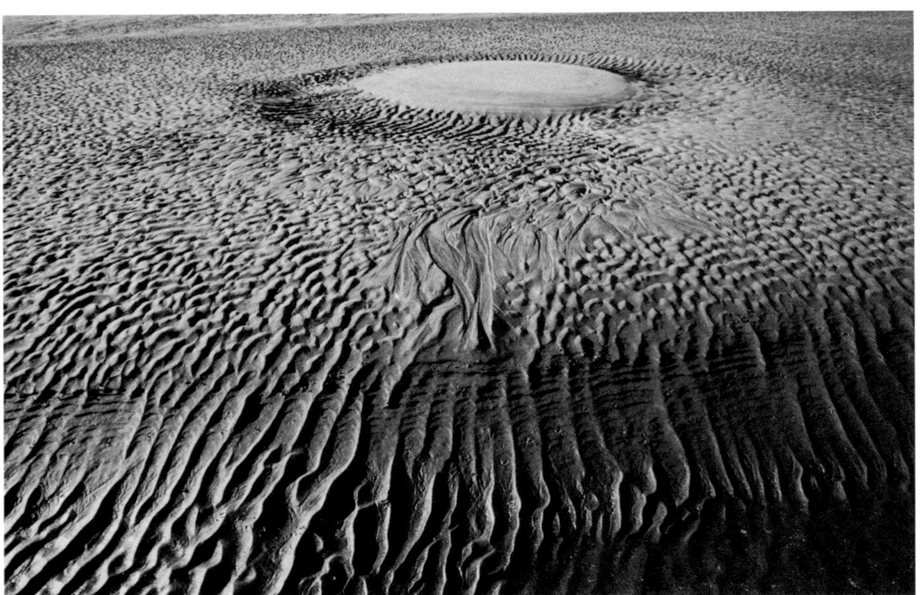

SANDS OF TIME #3
1997
Iris print
6⅝ x 10 inches

EDUCATION
1964-66 Columbia College, Columbia University,
New York

SELECTED SOLO EXHIBITIONS
1995   Kodak Gallery, Tokyo, Japan
1994   Light Sources, Boston
1993   Gallery 6, Tokyo

SELECTED GROUP EXHIBITIONS
1993-98 New Canaan Society for the Arts,
Connecticut
1996-97 Connections Gallery, Brunswick, Maine

The approach of the millennium offers us a special vantage point to reflect on time itself. Most people are conscious of how much more accelerated our sense of time is today, with the domination of electronic media, around-the-clock news, and tight deadlines. Many of my professional assignments as a photographer are based on recording fast-moving events. But I also try to focus, as a photographic artist, on something quite the opposite: to record the slow, relentless, and barely-seen passage of time.

The camera is an elegant time machine. It can freeze an instant, or capture the flow of time. Time is normally measured by the movement of the sun, the moon, and tides; it is fascinating that one of the earliest clocks, the hourglass, measured time by the flow of sand through a small constricted opening in a glass bottle—similar to the way a camera lens controls light passing through an adjustable aperture.

The *Sands of Time* is part of a long-term photographic project to make visible the flow of time as traced by tide and wind on the ever-changing surface of the beach. The short-lived and ephemeral patterns etched on the dynamic shoreline are fleeting, only to be erased by the next tide. Each is unique and yet somehow the same, like a moment in eternity.

ISLAND
1997
oil on linen
72 x 48 inches

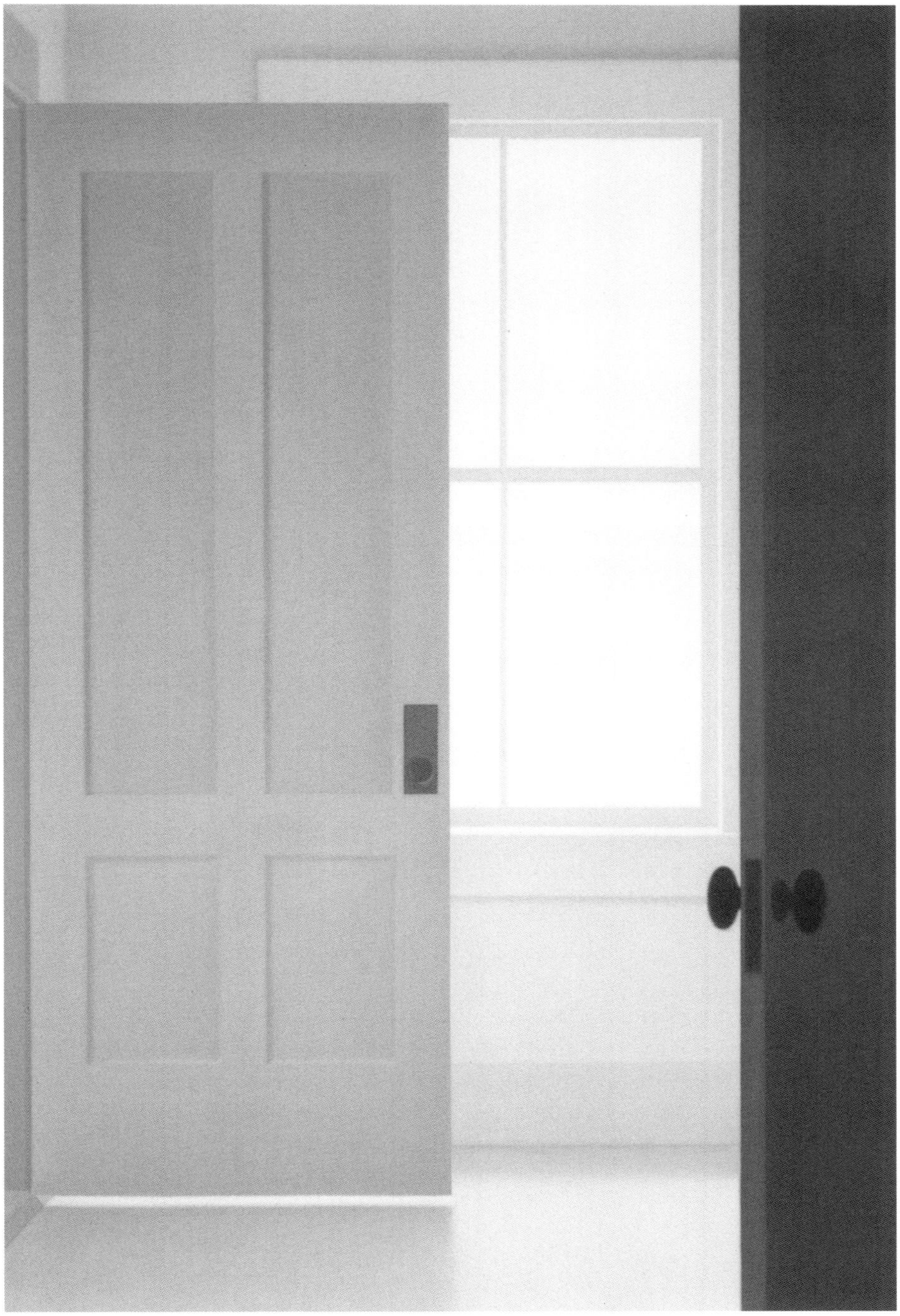

EDUCATION

1973   M.F.A., Painting, University of Miami, Florida
1971   B.F.A., Painting, University of Miami

HONORS AND AWARDS

1996   Pollock-Krasner Foundation Grant Award, New York
1996   National Endowment for the Arts Fellowship
1995   Artists Residency, The MacDowell Colony for the Arts, Peterborough, New Hampshire
1994   Purchase Award, American Academy of Arts and Letters, New York

SELECTED SOLO EXHIBITIONS

1997   Tatistcheff & Company, New York (also 1995, 1992)
1996   Icon Contemporary Art, Brunswick, Maine
1994   J.S. Ames Fine Art, Belfast, Maine

SELECTED GROUP EXHIBITIONS

1998   *Drawings IV,* Koplin Gallery, Los Angeles
1998   *After Dark,* Maine Coast Artists, Rockport
1997   *Re-Presenting Representation,* Arnot Art Museum, Elmira, New York
1996   *Degrees of Light: Paintings by Katherine Bradford and Mark Wethli,* Farnsworth Art Museum, Rockland, Maine
1996   *Reinventing Realism: Contemporary American Perspectives,* Everhart Museum, Scranton, Pennsylvania

SELECTED COLLECTIONS

- Portland Museum of Art, Maine
- Bowdoin College Museum of Art, Brunswick, Maine
- DeCordova Museum and Sculpture Park, Lincoln, Massachusetts
- Farnsworth Art Museum
- Metropolitan Museum of Art, New York

The subject matter of my work—spare, light-filled, and carefully composed images of architectural interiors—is intended as both a metaphorical image of stillness and a literal means of contemplation and clarity of mind. As in Buddhist meditation, Judeo-Christian and Islamic prayer, the Hindu mantra, and other means of introspective exercise, they are meant not simply as pictures but as a means of evoking a spiritual or metaphysical awareness.

LUCY WHITE

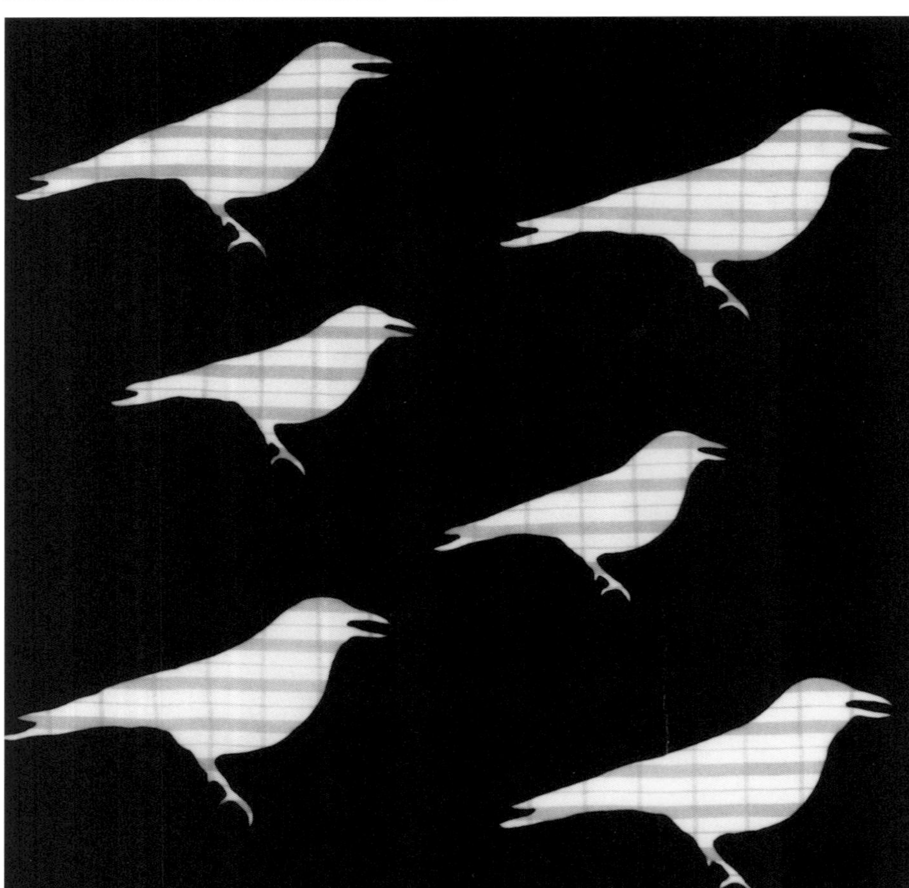

CROW
1997
dye, resin, and dishcloth on wood
23 x 23 x 2 inches

Familiar forms evoke a presence. Familiar products invoke a narrative. Dishcloths, Band-aids, and Handi-wipe towels, cut up and preserved in multiple layers of resin, contribute to new images but carry their old context. Lawns, houses, breasts, and crows resist the reduction to profile and pattern. Think of my latest work as a kind of inventory list, a lexicon of highly resonant and singular images. Recognizing this minimal vocabulary, the paintings can be strung together in simple sentences that describe a suburban landscape.

EDUCATION
1981   B.F.A., Minneapolis College of Art and Design, Minnesota

SELECTED SOLO EXHIBITIONS
1999   *Wholesome*, Bernard Toale Gallery, Boston
1998   *Synthetic Ecstasty*, Institute of Contemporary Art, Maine College of Art, Portland
1995   *New Paintings*, Bernard Toale Gallery
1992   *Taming Power of the Small*, Kimball Bourgault Gallery, Boston

SELECTED GROUP EXHIBITIONS
1998   *1998 DeCordova Annual Exhibition*, DeCordova Museum and Sculpture Park, Lincoln, Massachusetts
1998   *Depth and Illusion: Varieties of Abstract Space*, Gallery NAGA, Boston
1998   *Emblem*, Boston Center for the Arts, Mills Gallery, Massachusetts
1998   *Summer Group*, Albert Merola Gallery, Provincetown, Massachusetts
1997   *Synergy*, Robert Clements Gallery, Portland, Maine

SELECTED COLLECTIONS
- Fidelity Investments, Boston
- Neuberger and Berman, New York
- Wellington Management, Boston
- Rose Art Museum, Brandeis University, Waltham, Massachusetts
- AidsAction Inc., Boston

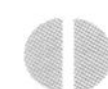

NEW APARTMENT
1996
oil on canvas
20½ x 25 inches

EDUCATION

1976   M.F.A., San Francisco Art Institute
1974   B.F.A., San Francisco Art Institute

SELECTED SOLO EXHIBITIONS

1996   *Richard Wilson—New Paintings,* June
Fitzpatrick Gallery, Portland, Maine
(also 1993)

SELECTED GROUP EXHIBITIONS

1998   *Gallery Artists,* June Fitzpatrick Gallery
1997   *PERSPECTIVES: The Art of the Book,*
Portland Museum of Art, Maine
1996   *Gallery Artists,* June Fitzpatrick Gallery
1995   *Winter's Work,* Frick Gallery, Belfast, Maine
1994   *Drawing to the Nth Degree,* Baxter Gallery,
Maine College of Art, Portland

SELECTED COLLECTIONS

- Portland Museum of Art
- University of Southern Maine, Gorham
- Sackler Library, Harvard University,
  Cambridge, Massachusetts
- Childrens Hospital, Cleveland, Ohio
- University of Maine School of Law, Portland

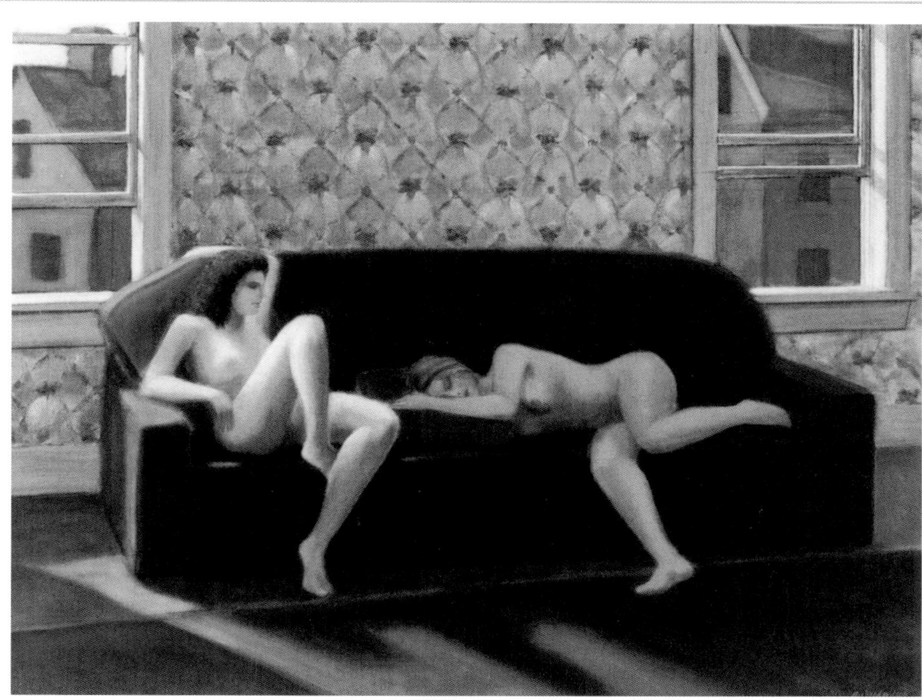

The subject of my artwork is inspired by observations I have made or situations I have been in. The viewer is a voyeur, glimpsing the moment I have created. I am interested in the mystery of private and familiar interactions seen from behind a door or across a room.

DUDLEY ZOPP

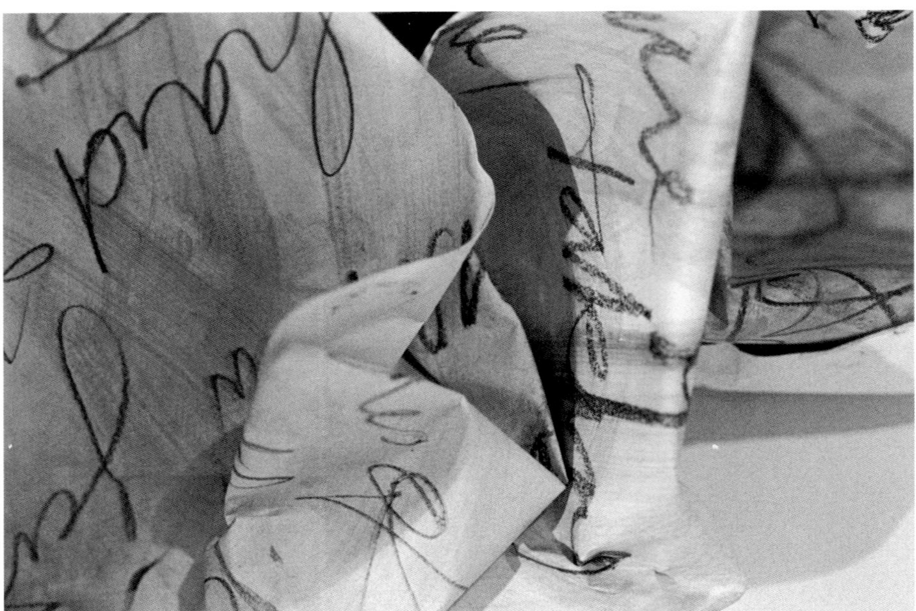

ERRATICS
1998
mixed media on paper
dimensions variable

I believe that the landscape is written, as books and letters are written. Though I seek to reveal particular landscapes, the act of translation allows infinite permutations—ways in which the landscape can be read, the trails followed, the art works constructed. Walking through my installations or reading my paintings and drawings is a lot like leafing through a book for answers, or turning a kaleidoscope until the bits fall into place. We scan to look for meanings, symbols, and delineations, try to create order out of a confusion of information. There are moments of clarity in the forest as well as in the gallery, when our attention is caught and held, when we can almost crack the code and say, yes! now I understand how the natural world speaks and what it says.

The evolutionary nature of landscape leads me to choose materials which are semi-permanent, and to create installations which are ephemeral. Paper and wood are the structural media; obscured words and calligraphic brush marks are applied in a variety of pigments, graphite, charcoal, and shellac. Twisted three-dimensional constructions convey the effects of wind and water and the morphological qualities of rock. The architecture of the exhibition space is the starting point for the configurations of the constructions. Works placed along shifting horizon lines, from floor to ceiling, create a new landscape for the viewer to walk through, a landscape where we learn to listen with our eyes.

EDUCATION

1986-91 Post-Graduate Studies in Drawing and Painting, Allen R. Hite Art Institute, University of Louisville, Kentucky
1964 M.A., University of Kentucky, Lexington
1963 B.A., Foreign Languages, University of Kentucky

HONORS AND AWARDS

1997 Studio Residency, Pouch Cove Foundation, Saint John's, Newfoundland

SELECTED SOLO EXHIBITIONS

1998 *Reading the Landscape,* UMF Art Gallery, University of Maine, Farmington
1997 *Erratics,* Maine Coast Artists, Rockport
1997 Spring Street Gallery, Belfast, Maine
1997 *Drawings from Newfoundland,* Bank One Gallery, Louisville
1996 *The Rumpelstiltskin Letters,* Spalding University, Louisville

SELECTED GROUP EXHIBITIONS

1998 *New To Town,* Davidson & Daughters Contemporary Art, Portland, Maine
1998 *What Women Experience,* University of Maine at Machias
1998 *Fifty for Fifty,* Pegasus Gallery, Louisville
1997 *Paperwork,* Maine Coast Artists
1997 Between The Muse Gallery, Rockland, Maine

SELECTED COLLECTIONS

- Bell South Mobility, Louisville
- National Processing Corporation, Louisville
- Commonwealth Bank and Trust, Middletown, Kentucky
- Cumberland College, Williamsburg, Kentucky
- NOXBOX, Mainz, Germany

EXHIBITION CHECKLIST 

Artists are listed alphabetically. Dimensions are in inches, height preceding width.

For artists with more than one piece on view, an asterisk (*) indicates the catalogue illustration.

MARY ARMSTRONG
Dante's Woods #2, 1995-97
oil on panel
60 x 48
Lent by the artist

MARY ARO
*Hunters Beach, Acadia**, 1997
watercolor on paper
12 x 16
Lent by the artist

Hunters Beach, 1997
watercolor on paper
12 x 16
Lent by the artist

JUNE AUGUST
Target III, 1996
monotype
180 x 144
Lent by the artist

JEFFERY BECTON
*Anticipating Ascension**, 1997
Iris print
16 x 23
Lent by the artist

Looking West, 1996
Iris print
25 x 28
Lent by the artist

TODD BERNARD
Dichotomy, 1998
marker on wood
42 x 42
Lent by the artist

BRETT BIGBEE
Bird I, 1998
graphite on paper
48¼ x 28¼
Lent by Tibor de Nagy Gallery

JOHN BISBEE
*Husk**, 1997
welded nails
22 x 48 x 42
Lent by the artist

Field, 1998
welded nails
24 x 24 x 24 inches
Lent by the artist

Ring, 1998
welded nails
51 x 21 x 51
Lent by the artist

PRILLA SMITH BRACKETT
Remnants: Communion # 8, 1998
acrylic wash, graphite, conté,
charcoal, pastel, and collage
on paper
26¼ x 34⅛
Lent by the artist

ALAN BRAY
*Vernal Pond**, 1997
casein on panel
26 x 34
Lent by William Farley

Blackbirds, 1997
casein on panel
17 x 22
Lent by William Muchnic

SAM CADY
*Two Shaker Buildings, Early
Evening,* 1998
oil on shaped canvas
62 x 67 x 1½
Lent by the artist, courtesy of
Mary Ryan Gallery, New York

DAVID CAMPBELL
The Family, 1996-98
charcoal, conté, and graphite
on paper
33 x 40
Lent by the artist

PATRICIA CAMPBELL
Constructed Form (Lotus), 1998
rice paper and reed
62 x 34 x 4
Lent by the artist

Samurai, 1996
rice paper and reed
54 x 32 x 6
Lent by the artist

ELIZABETH CASHIN MCMILLEN
Untitled No. 20, 1996
oil on canvas
92 x 72
Lent by the artist

TOM CHAPIN
Cage, 1998
black marble and dinosaur
bone resin
17 x 15¼ x 8½
Lent by the artist

Birthstone, 1998
Indian black granite
6½ x 12⅞ x 10
Lent by the artist

PAUL D'AMATO
Bridge Players, Woodford's Club, Portland, 1997
c-print
30 x 36
Lent by the artist

Girl on Swing, Chicago, 1997
c-print
30 x 36
Lent by the artist

GRACE DeGENNARO
Pinnate #1, 1997
oil on linen
22 x 18 x 2
Private collection

Hourglass (For P.D.), 1997
oil on linen
22 x 18 x 2
Lent by the artist

RUDOLPH DE HARAK
Union River Bay 7, 1998
acrylic on linen
43 x 37 x 2½
Lent by the artist

FRITZ DIETEL
Burr, 1997
cypress and mixed media
120 x 28 x 28
Lent by the artist

BEVIN ENGMAN
Bellow's Edge, 1997
oil on wood
12 x 12
Lent by the artist

Dissembling Sheath, 1997
oil on wood
12¾ x 12¾
Private collection

RICH ENTEL
Voice, 1997
oil and metal leaf on wood
72 x 72
Lent by the artist, courtesy of
Caldbeck Gallery, Rockland, Maine

DON GORVETT
The Tarr and Wonson Copper Paint Manufactory, 1997
seven color reduction woodcut on
Okawara paper
34 x 26
Lent by the artist

ERIC GREEN
Pool, 1996
oil on canvas
40 x 65
Lent by Gallery Henoch

MARTHA GROOME
Over Blue, 1998
acrylic on canvas
28 x 28
Lent by the artist

TOM HALL
Ring Farm, 1996
mixed media on paper
6 x 6 x 1½ i
Lent by the artist

McAuley Orchard, 1996
mixed media on paper
6 x 6 x 1½
Lent by Peter Holmes

TONEE HARBERT
Flight III, 1996
gelatin silver print
16 x 20
Lent by the artist

Flight VI, 1996
gelatin silver print
20 x 16
Lent by the artist

DEWITT HARDY
Winter Nap, 1997
watercolor on paper
18 x 30
Lent by Mast Cove Gallery,
Kennebunkport, Maine

Self Portrait, 1998
watercolor on paper
12 x 18
Lent by the artist

ANNE HARRIS
Second Portrait with Max, 1996-97
oil on canvas
46 x 30
Lent by The Estabrook Foundation,
courtesy of Nielsen Gallery, Boston

Max Newborn, 1996
oil on masonite
6½ x 5¼
Lent by Paul D'Amato

Max Newborn, Face and Hands,
1996
oil on masonite
3⅛ x 2½
Lent by Bruce Brown

DANIEL HEYMAN
On the Way to Fred's, 1998
gouache on paper
54 x 45
Lent by the artist

TAMAKI HONDA
*Attempt 1**, 1997
oil and wax on masonite
36 x 36
Lent by the artist

Attempt 2, 1997
oil and wax on masonite
48 x 48
Lent by the artist

SHERRILL EDWARDS HUNNIBELL
*Book of Hours #44:
Groping in the Dark**, 1996
mixed media altered book
6 x 9¼ x 1¼
Lent by the artist

*Book of Hours #46: Half-Melted
and Pale*, 1996
mixed media altered book
6¼ x 8 x ½ x ¾
Lent by the artist

CONSTANCE KIERMAIER
The Forest, 1997-98
mixed media on wood
84 x variable x ¾
Lent by the artist

EUGENE KOCH
*Sea Smoke #15**, 1997
India ink on clayboard
24 x 24
Lent by the artist

Sea Smoke #16, 1997
India ink on clayboard
24 x 36
Lent by the artist

MICHAEL H. LEWIS
*Clearing**, 1997
turpentine wash on paper
28 x 38
Lent by the artist

Prayer for Peace #6, 1996
turpentine wash on paper
8 x 12
Lent by the artist

THOMAS LIBBEY
*Cyclette #13**, 1998
gelatin silver print
18½ x 22½
Lent by the artist

Cyclette #14, 1998
gelatin silver print
18½ x 22½
Lent by the artist

GEORGE LLOYD
L'Acquaiòla, 1997
oil on canvas
20 x 16
Lent by the artist

*Summer Rev**, 1997
oil on plywood
24 x 20
Lent by the Artist

GARRY MITCHELL
*Untitled 2**, 1998
alkyd and wax on canvas
20 x 16
Private collection

Untitled 6, 1998
alkyd and wax on canvas
30 x 24
Lent by the artist

ROBERT ERIC MOORE
*Island Near Owl's Head**, 1997
watercolor on paper
14½ x 21
Lent by the artist

Vaughan Island off Turbot's Creek,
1997
watercolor on paper
14½ x 21
Lent by the artist

BARBARA PETTER PUTNAM
Prairie Storm, Manitoba, 1997
woodcut on paper
24 x 48
Lent by the artist

NEAL RANTOUL
*Near Colfax, Washington (8)**, 1996
dye coupler print
40 x 48
Lent by the artist

Near Colfax, Washington (9), 1996
dye coupler print
40 x 48
Lent by the artist

LORNA J. RITZ
Light and Shadow on Snow, 1998
oil on linen
48 x 60
Lent by the artist

CELESTE ROBERGE
Stack, 1998
antique chaise lounge and slate
48 x 72 x 27
Lent by the artist

LIV KRISTIN ROBINSON
*Belfast Waterfront (#5)**, 1996
oil pigment on toned gelatin
silver print
22 x 24
Lent by the artist

Belfast Waterfront (#6), 1996
oil pigment on toned gelatin
silver print
22 x 24
Lent by the artist

● EXHIBITION CHECKLIST

ABBY SHAHN
Twelve Corners, 1996
egg tempera on panels
30 x 90
Lent by the artist, courtesy of
Caldbeck Gallery

MICHAEL SHAUGHNESSY
*Pomoni's Loop and Fall, Second
Variation,* 1998
hay and twine
120 x 72 x 36
Lent by the artist

SARAH M. SLAVICK
Tongue,* 1997
oil on wood
36 x 36
Lent by the artist

Tongue 2, 1997
oil on wood
36 x 36
Lent by the artist

ROBERT SOLOTAIRE
138th St. Bridge, 1996
oil on paper
18 x 30
Lent by the artist

GAIL SPAIEN
*The Struggle Between the Intellect
and the Spirit: Untitled,* 1998
acrylic on panel
18 x 18
Lent by the artist

*The Struggle Between the Intellect
and the Spirit: Just Before
Deciding*,* 1997
acrylic on panel
18 x 18
Lent by the artist

ALICE SPENCER
Fragment with Circles, 1998
plaster and acrylic on board
12 x 12 x 2½
Lent by the artist

Fragment with Green Stripe,* 1998
plaster and acrylic on board
12 x 12 x 2½
Lent by the artist

MARY ALICE TREWORGY
Ben's Bike,* 1997
oil on canvas
12 x 12
Lent by AM and John Goldkrand

Painting Concord, MA Barn, 1996
oil on canvas
14 x 14
Lent by the artist, courtesy of
Gleason Fine Art, Portland, Maine

FRANK VALLIERE
Start Me Up, 1997
oil pastel on paper
14 x 17
Lent by the artist

ROBERT VAN VRANKEN
*Untitled (The Empty Cup Runneth
Over),* 1998
oil on board
48 x 36
Lent by the artist

DAVID WADE
Sands of Time #1, 1997
Iris print
6⅝ x 10
Lent by the artist

Sands of Time #3,* 1997
Iris print
6⅝ x 10
Lent by the artist

MARK WETHLI
Island,* 1997
oil on linen
72 x 48
Lent by Tatistcheff and Company,
Inc., New York

Flight, 1997
oil on linen
72 x 48
Lent by Tatistcheff and Company,
Inc., New York

LUCY WHITE
Crow,* 1997
dye, resin, and dishcloth on wood
23 x 23 x 2
Lent by the artist, courtesy of Robert
Clements Gallery, Portland, Maine

Handi-Wipe Houses, 1997
blue Handi-wipes, resin, and
acrylic on wood
23 x 23 x 2
Lent by the artist, courtesy of Robert
Clements Gallery, Portland, Maine

RICHARD A. WILSON
New Apartment, 1996
oil on canvas
20½ x 25
Private collection

DUDLEY ZOPP
Erratics, 1998
mixed media on paper
dimensions variable
Lent by the artist